Poptropica®

THE OFFICIAL GUIDE

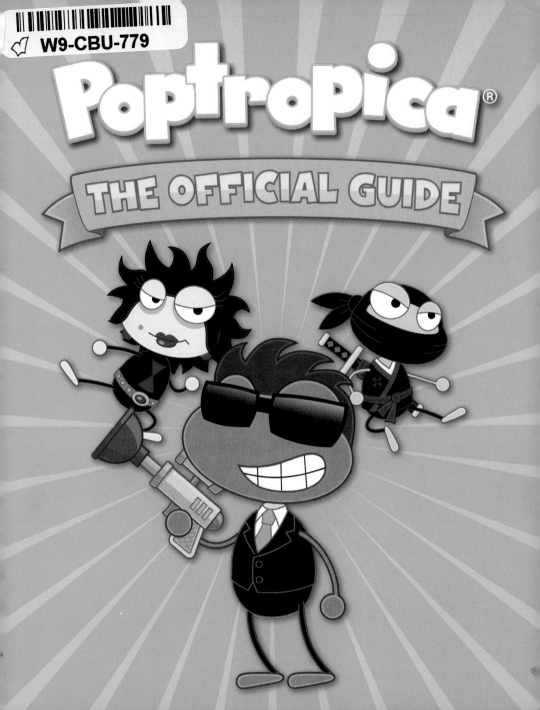

by Tracey West
cover designed by Nate Greenwall

Poptropica
An Imprint of Penguin Group (USA) Inc.

POPTROPICA
PUBLISHED BY THE PENGUIN GROUP
PENGUIN GROUP (USA) INC., 375 HUDSON STREET, NEW YORK, NEW YORK 10014, USA
PENGUIN GROUP (CANADA), 90 EGLINTON AVENUE EAST, SUITE 700,
TORONTO, ONTARIO M4P 2Y3, CANADA
(A DIVISION OF PEARSON PENGUIN CANADA INC.)
PENGUIN BOOKS LTD., 80 STRAND, LONDON WC2R 0RL, ENGLAND
PENGUIN GROUP IRELAND, 25 ST. STEPHEN'S GREEN, DUBLIN 2, IRELAND
(A DIVISION OF PENGUIN BOOKS LTD.)
PENGUIN GROUP (AUSTRALIA), 250 CAMBERWELL ROAD,
CAMBERWELL, VICTORIA 3124, AUSTRALIA
(A DIVISION OF PEARSON AUSTRALIA GROUP PTY. LTD.)
PENGUIN BOOKS INDIA PVT. LTD., 11 COMMUNITY CENTRE,
PANCHSHEEL PARK, NEW DELHI–110 017, INDIA
PENGUIN GROUP (NZ), 67 APOLLO DRIVE, ROSEDALE, AUCKLAND 0632, NEW ZEALAND
(A DIVISION OF PEARSON NEW ZEALAND LTD.)
PENGUIN BOOKS (SOUTH AFRICA) (PTY.) LTD., 24 STURDEE AVENUE,
ROSEBANK, JOHANNESBURG 2196, SOUTH AFRICA

PENGUIN BOOKS LTD., REGISTERED OFFICES: 80 STRAND, LONDON WC2R 0RL, ENGLAND

WELCOME TO POPTROPICA

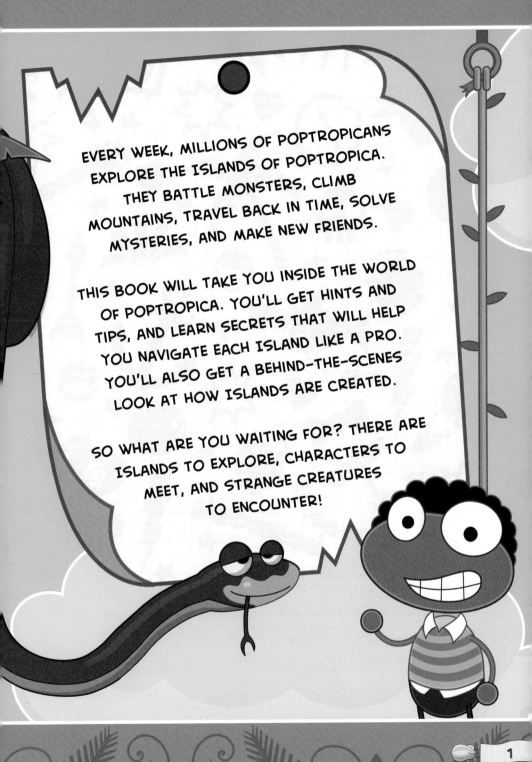

EVERY WEEK, MILLIONS OF POPTROPICANS EXPLORE THE ISLANDS OF POPTROPICA. THEY BATTLE MONSTERS, CLIMB MOUNTAINS, TRAVEL BACK IN TIME, SOLVE MYSTERIES, AND MAKE NEW FRIENDS.

THIS BOOK WILL TAKE YOU INSIDE THE WORLD OF POPTROPICA. YOU'LL GET HINTS AND TIPS, AND LEARN SECRETS THAT WILL HELP YOU NAVIGATE EACH ISLAND LIKE A PRO. YOU'LL ALSO GET A BEHIND-THE-SCENES LOOK AT HOW ISLANDS ARE CREATED.

SO WHAT ARE YOU WAITING FOR? THERE ARE ISLANDS TO EXPLORE, CHARACTERS TO MEET, AND STRANGE CREATURES TO ENCOUNTER!

TABLE OF CONTENTS

IN THE BEGINNING . . .

CURIOUS ADVENTURERS FIRST BEGAN TO DISCOVER POPTROPICA IN THE YEAR 2007. THESE EXPLORERS TRAVELED BY BLIMP TO HOP FROM ISLAND TO ISLAND. THEY SOON NOTICED SOMETHING STRANGE AND WONDERFUL: JUST WHEN THEY THOUGHT THEIR JOURNEY WAS OVER, A NEW ISLAND WOULD APPEAR.

EXACTLY WHAT POPTROPICA IS AND WHAT IT WILL BECOME IS NOT YET UNDERSTOOD. BUT THAT'S WHAT ADVENTURERS LIKE BEST ABOUT IT— EXPLORING THE UNKNOWN!

MAP OF THE ISLANDS

WHEN YOU FIRST ENTER POPTROPICA, YOU'LL BE TAKEN TO
A MAP SHOWING ALL THE ISLANDS YOU CAN EXPLORE.

EARLY POPTROPICA

MYTHOLOGY island

SHARK TOOTH ISLAND

CHOOSE YOUR OWN ADVENTURE®
NABOOTI ISLAND

SALOON

WILD WEST island

Wimpy WONDERLAND

Reality TV island

ASTRO KNIGHTS ISLAND

ptropica

TIME TANGLED
ISLAND

SPY
ISLAND

big
NATE
ISLAND

SUPER POWER ISLAND

cryptids
ISLAND

STEAMWORKS
ISLAND

24 CARROT ISLAND

WELCOME
GREAT
PUMPKIN

Great Pumpkin
Island

SKULLDUGGERY
ISLAND

COUNTERFEIT
ISLAND

GETTING AROUND POPTROPICA

BEFORE YOU START ISLAND-HOPPING, YOU MIGHT WANT TO KNOW HOW STUFF WORKS. IN THIS SECTION, YOU'LL FIND TIPS FOR MOVING AROUND AND WILL LEARN WHAT THOSE ICONS ON THE TOP OF YOUR SCREEN MEAN.

CREATE YOUR AVATAR

When you first enter the Poptropica site, you'll be asked to create a character. If it's your first time, click on New Player. Click on boy or girl, and then click on your age. *Presto!* Your character will pop up, along with your character name.

Want a new look? Click on Change Character to give yourself a makeover. If you want to start from scratch and get a new name, click Change All.

When you're happy with how you look, click on the balloon to start playing. It's that simple!

ENTER

WELCOME

Lone Lightning

CHANGE ALL ▶
SKIN COLOR ▶
HAIR ▶
HAIR COLOR ▶
EYES ▶
MOUTH ▶
SHIRT ▶
PANTS ▶

CHOOSE AN ISLAND

The balloon will take you to the Poptropica Map. Use your cursor to move around and check out the different Islands. Click on the Island you want to explore.

KNOW YOUR ICONS

As soon as you enter an Island, a row of icons will pop up on the top right of your screen:

BLIMP

Click on this icon to leave any page and get back to your game.

THE DAILY POP

Click on Pop, and you'll see three tabs: Comics, Games, and Sneak Peeks. In the Comics section, you can read some of your favorite syndicated comic strips. Go to the Games section to play mini-games you won't find anywhere else on the site. Compete against other Poptropicans and see if you can get the high score of the day. And in Sneak Peeks you'll see sketches and other artwork from upcoming Poptropica Islands.

STATS/STORE

If you click on the green coin, you'll find yourself in the Poptropica Store. Here you can use Credits to buy Gold Cards or costumes. You can get Credits for free when you create a username and finish an Island. You can also buy Credits (with an adult's permission). If you get a Membership, you won't need Credits because everything's free for Members.

CLASSIC FLAVOR
POPGUM

FREE

Press SPACEBAR to blow bubbles.

CHEW

Each Gold Card is different. Some of them contain cool items your character can have fun with, like Popgum. Others let you become invisible, visit new places, or even change the look of another character you meet.

TIP:
Check the Poptropica Store frequently to see what new Gold Cards are out—some of them are free!

At the top of this page you'll see another tab marked Stats. Each time you complete an Island, you'll earn a Medallion. You can find those Medallions here. You'll also see how many Credits you have and be able to check your battle ranking. You can increase this ranking by visiting multi-player rooms and challenging Poptropicans to the different games available there. You will find multi-player rooms on every Island you visit.

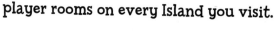

USING A GOLD CARD

1. CLICK ON THE SUITCASE ICON TO OPEN UP YOUR ITEMS. GO TO *STORE ITEMS*. CLICK ON THE CARD YOU WANT TO USE.
2. EACH CARD HAS AN ACTION YOU CAN PERFORM IN A WHITE BAR ON THE BOTTOM. TO USE CLASSIC FLAVOR POPGUM, CLICK *CHEW*. THEN CLICK ON *CLOSE* TO LEAVE YOUR ITEM'S SUITCASE.
3. YOUR CHARACTER WILL START CHEWING GUM! FOLLOW THE INSTRUCTIONS ON THE CARD TO BLOW BUBBLES—PRESS DOWN ON YOUR SPACEBAR.
4. TO STOP CHEWING, OPEN UP YOUR ITEMS AGAIN AND CLICK ON THE CARD. THEN CLICK ON *STOP CHEWING*.

ITEMS

Once you get something in a game or buy it in the Poptropica Store, you will find it in Store Items. Click on the suitcase icon to access your items. If you are on an Island, the items from that Island will appear on your screen. To access your other items, click on the blue bar on the top left of your screen and scroll down.

Click on Store Items to use stuff you got from the Poptropica Store. You'll see ten cards per page—click on the bottom right to see a new page of items. When you find the card you want to use, click on it and follow the instructions. Click on Close on the top right to exit your items suitcase.

While you are exploring an Island, you might need to use one of the items you've found. Usually, the item will appear exactly when you need it. At other times, you may need to click on the card to use it.

CHANGE YOUR LOOK WITH COSTUMES

1. USE CREDITS OR A MEMBERSHIP TO PURCHASE A COSTUME IN THE POPTROPICA STORE. THERE ARE DOZENS TO CHOOSE FROM!
2. OPEN YOUR ITEMS FOLDER AND CLICK ON THE COSTUME CARD. THEN CLICK ON COSTUMIZE.
3. DO YOU WANT TO CREATE A LOOK THAT'S PART ZOMBIE, PART NINJA, AND PART PROM QUEEN? NO PROBLEM! YOU CAN USE ALL OF A COSTUME OR JUST PARTS OF IT. CLICK ON EACH PIECE TO CHOOSE THE ONES YOU WANT.

MAP

Click on the Map icon to see a Map of the Island you're on. It's a useful feature if you're lost or confused. The Map will always show your current location. New locations will appear after you discover them.

COSTUMIZER

Maybe you dig the cool sunglasses another character is wearing. Or you covet that sword they're carrying. You can use the Costumizer to copy just about any look you love!

When you click on the green shirt icon, you'll see the words *Select Character*. Click on a character whose look you want to copy. It can be a character from the game or another player you meet in a multi-player room. A screen will pop up. Click on the items you want to wear, and they'll appear on your character.

There's one catch: Items you swipe using the Costumizer do not end up in your Inventory. Once you take them off, they're gone—until you Costumize them again.

This symbol takes you to your personal home page. You'll end up here when you sign back into your account!

GET MOVING

Once you're ready to start exploring the Island, you'll need to move left, right, up, down, over, and under obstacles in your way. Here are some tips to help you get around.

1. When you see 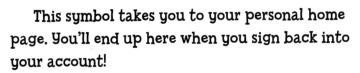, you can move left or right. Click once to take one step. Keep clicking to walk. Your speed is determined by the distance of the cursor from your character while you're holding the mouse button. The farther the arrow, the faster you'll move.

2. When you see , you can jump. Jump on top of objects to get over them. If the arrow is pointing down, you'll jump down.

3. You can climb things like ropes, vines, and pipes by clicking on them. Hold down your cursor to shimmy up and down them.

mike's

USEFUL STUFF

★ **Create an Account:** The first time you play, you'll need to create a username and password to save your game. Always remember to write down your password, and never share your password with anybody but a parent.

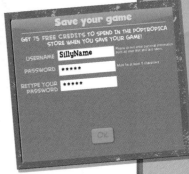

★ **Save Your Game:**
Before you leave Poptropica, click on *Save* on the bottom right of your screen. If you don't, you may have to start your adventure all over again!

★ **Chat with Characters:** As you roam the Islands, you'll meet many Island inhabitants. They will have useful information for you. To chat with a character, click on him or her. A speech bubble will appear over the character's head. If the character is important to the story of the Island, you may have a conversation with him or her. When you click on the character, questions will appear above your head. Click on each question you want to ask and wait for the character's answer.

USEFUL STUFF

★ **Chat with Other Players:** When you are in a multi-player room, you can use safe chat to talk to other players. Click on the player you want to talk to. Then select *Chat*. Three speech balloons will appear above your head. Click on the balloon

you want to use. Then wait for your answer. You can also click on one of the face icons on the right to express how you're feeling. You can smile, laugh, cry, or get angry.

★ **Battle Other Players:** Click on a player in a multi-player room if you want to battle. Then click on *Battle*. A selection of games to play will appear above your head. Click on one to ask the player if they want to play with you. Then wait for a response. If another player asks you to battle, you can accept the challenge or turn them down.

EXPLORE THE ISLANDS

YOUR POPTROPICA ADVENTURE STARTS BY HOPPING ON A BLIMP AND SOARING OVER A SEA OF ISLANDS. WHEN YOU VISIT AN ISLAND, IT'S LIKE OPENING THE FIRST PAGE OF A BOOK. THERE'S A GREAT STORY THERE, WAITING TO BE UNCOVERED. BUT IN POPTROPICA, YOU'RE THE MAIN CHARACTER EVERY TIME!

Each Island has its own set of challenges to complete. When you complete all the challenges successfully, you will earn a Medallion for that Island. In this section, we'll walk you through the action on each Island and introduce you to the characters you'll meet there. Look for hints, tips, and secrets to help you master your game.

If you're just starting out, Early Poptropica and Shark Tooth Island are the perfect Islands for getting used to how the challenges work. After enjoying these two Islands, you'll be ready to dive into any Island with both feet!

EARLY POPTROPICA

DIFFICULTY: EASY

SYNOPSIS: EARLY POPTROPICA WAS THE VERY FIRST ISLAND TO APPEAR IN POPTROPICA. ON IT, THE ISLAND'S OLDEST INHABITANTS ASK YOU TO HELP THEM LOCATE THREE STOLEN ITEMS: A PIG, A BUCKET, AND A SIGNAL FLAG.

FIRST STOP: MAIN STREET

When you climb down from the blimp, you'll find yourself on Main Street. Go inside the Pop Art Museum to see art from famous artists and speak to the artists themselves. Meet other players inside the two multi-player rooms: the Soda Pop Shop and the Arcade.

You could start exploring by climbing up the Water Tower. You'll see a flag there, but you won't be able to reach it. You'll also see an open manhole. You can jump down now if you want, but you might want to wait until you get your Glow Stick. Getting back up isn't so easy!

THE OLD PART OF TOWN

Go right on Main Street to get to Early Poptropica. The characters here look like pilgrims, and the buildings look like old cabins. If you talk to these early inhabitants, they'll tell you about the items they're missing: One pilgrim is missing a Pig, one is missing a Bucket, and the third is missing a Signal Flag.

Remember that Glow Stick we mentioned? You can find it here if you climb down inside the well and jump from platform to platform. Walk into the Glow Stick to add it to your items.

TIP:
To find the last pilgrim, go all the way to the end of the dock and climb up the rope hanging down from the watchtower.

"THE EIGHT-BIT CHARACTERS YOU'LL FIND IN EARLY POPTROPICA ARE A REFERENCE TO OLD-SCHOOL GAMING."
—SHARK BOY

BACK TO MAIN STREET

Now that you have the Glow Stick, it's time to explore that manhole. Jump down to the very bottom. You might get knocked over by a spider, but that's okay. Even if you fall all the way to the bottom, you'll still land on your feet. Then jump over the green spider and move right to find the prized porker. Touch the

pig to add it to your items. You might be tempted to leave the manhole now, but there's more to be found down there. Get past the green spider again and enter the tunnel on your left.

TIP:
Those purple spiders can knock you back to the ground if you're not careful. Time your jumps to avoid the spiders when they fall.

Your Glow Stick will light the way through the tunnel. When you see a rope, climb up. Keep climbing until you find the Golden Egg. There are hints written on the walls to tell you if you're going in the right direction. When you find the Golden Egg, touch it to add it to your items.

After you get the Egg, travel upward to find an exit, and you'll find yourself in front of Poptropica Towers.

CHECK OUT POPTROPICA TOWERS

So now you have the Pig, but you still need the Bucket and the Flag. Since you're at Poptropica Towers, you should start exploring the city street lined with tall buildings. Jump to the ledge of the first building you see and head for the roof! Travel from rooftop to rooftop, bouncing off clotheslines to help you. When you reach the blue building, climb to the very top, which looks like a rooftop restaurant. Then climb up the vine.

LAND OF THE PURPLE GIANT

Now you're in the clouds. Move right until you see a huge pair of purple feet. Click on them to talk to the giant. He'll accept your Golden Egg as payment to enter his vegetable garden. You'll find the bucket among the enormous veggies.

ENTER THE AIRCRAFT GRAVEYARD

Keep moving right until you find the Aircraft Graveyard. You can't use any of the planes here, but if you look carefully, you'll find a Jet Pack. This is just what you need to get to high places—like the top of the Water Tower, where the Signal Flag awaits you.

Get back to Main Street any way you can. Then use the Jet Pack to fly to the top of the Water Tower. To fly, move your cursor until you see a green up-arrow. Click and hold to move up. Then move left or right. When you reach the top of the tower, click on the Flag to add it to your items.

FYI: The Jet Pack is a great way to get around, but you can only use it while you are in Early Poptropica.

MAKE YOUR DELIVERIES

Now you've got the Pig, the Bucket, and the Flag.
Head back to Early Poptropica. (You can fly if you want
to, but you'll have to walk between Main Street and Early
Poptropica.)

   Talk to each of the three pilgrims who were missing items.
When you do, the items will be removed from your Inventory
and returned to their original owners. Once you return the
Signal Flag, a boat will reach the dock. Talk to the person on
the boat, and he will thank you with an Early
Poptropica Medallion. Congratulations!

TIP:

To wear your
Medallion, click on the
items icon. Click on the
Medallion card and click
on Put On. You can take it
off whenever you want by
returning to the card and
clicking on Take Off.

SHARK TTH ISLAND

DIFFICULTY: EASY
SYNOPSIS: THIS TROPICAL PARADISE IS
TERRORIZED BY A REAL MONSTER—A GIANT
SHARK NAMED THE GREAT BOOGA. YOU'LL
NEED TO GET PAST THE SHARK TO RESCUE
A LOST BOY—BUT HOW? A MYSTERIOUS
MEDICINE MAN MAY HAVE THE ANSWER YOU NEED.

FIRST STOP: MAIN STREET

The first thing you'll see when you walk down the dock
is a giant shark idol and a small souvenir stand. Talk to the
seller and he'll give you a Shark Fin. You won't need this to
complete the Island, but it's a sharp fashion accessory.

Keep going right and you'll
see the Coconut Café, a
multi-player room. Outside,
a guy with a ukulele is selling
Carbonated Coconut Milk.
Talk to him, and he'll add it
to your Inventory.

Next you'll find the Tourism Center, where you can read about the legend of the Great Booga. You'll also see a statue of Professor Hammerhead, a shark expert who's been lost at sea since 1997.

TIP:

On any Island, it's a good idea to explore the rooms on Main Street before you embark on your adventure. The things you learn will help you get into the story and, usually, give you clues that will help you in other places on the Island.

In the Shark Museum, you can learn about sharks. You'll also find Professor Hammerhead's Journal, which is missing some pages. Jump down into the shark pool to talk to one of the most famous characters in the Poptropica universe: Shark Boy.

WHO IS SHARK BOY?

INSIDE THE SHARK MUSEUM YOU'LL FIND A POOL THAT'S SUPPOSED TO HOLD A GREAT WHITE SHARK. IF YOU DIVE IN, YOU WON'T FIND THAT MAJESTIC BEAST—INSTEAD, YOU'LL FIND A GRUMPY BOY WEARING A CHEAP SHARK COSTUME. HE DOESN'T SEEM AT ALL HAPPY WITH HIS JOB.

HE'S A MINOR CHARACTER IN THE STORY OF THE ISLAND, BUT FANS OF POPTROPICA QUICKLY BECAME OBSESSED WITH SHARK BOY. THESE DAYS YOU'LL FIND SHARK BOY WRITING A POPULAR BLOG ON THE SITE. HE'S THE ALTER EGO OF ONE OF POPTROPICA'S CREATORS.

Once you leave the museum, keep going right to get to the Ancient Ruins. You'll find crumbling statues and an old temple dedicated to the Great Booga. There is a woman standing by the temple who will tell you that she lost a page from Professor Hammerhead's Journal, and the wind blew it up to the roof. You'll need that Journal Page to complete your quest.

Keep going right and you'll find a large stone block. Push the block to the big tree, underneath a dangling vine. Hop up on the block and climb up the vine. Jump to the first platform, then the second. Then make a big jump to the left. You'll land on the temple roof, where you will find the missing Journal Page.

If you go back to the vine and keep climbing up the tree, you will find the Medicine Man. Save yourself a trip and head to Booga Bay first. The Medicine Man won't help you unless you have a Grass Skirt, and that's where you'll find one.

TIP:
You can explore the temple now if you want, but you might want to wait until after you talk to the Medicine Man.

Keep going right to get to Booga Bay. Talk to the man at the Grass Skirt stand and he'll give you one. Put it on so you look like a native Islander. Keep going toward the shore, and you'll meet a woman who says her son is at sea, trapped by a giant shark!

You can jump in the water if you want to help. First you'll come to an Island. A fisherman will tell you that it's not safe to swim. That's because the Great Booga lives in the waters to the right of the Island. You can try feeding coconuts to the giant shark at this point, but you'll find it impossible to get past him.

There's only one way to go now—back to the Ancient Ruins.

INSIDE THE TEMPLE OF RUINS

Climb back up the tall tree, and at the very top you'll find the Medicine Man. If you're wearing your Grass Skirt,

he'll talk to you and tell you that he can make a Potion that will calm the Great Booga. You'll find a list of ingredients you'll need in the Temple of Ruins.

The temple is a dark and spooky place populated with purple fruit bats that will knock you down if they fly into you. Make your way to the bottom and head left. Then jump back up until you land on a swinging platform. Jump left and you'll end up on a landing next to a panel with a secret code on it. It's the same as the code from Professor Hammerhead's Journal!

Since you have the missing Journal Page, you know what to do: Click on the symbols to spell *O-P-E-N*. Then click on the triangle, and the hidden panel will open for you.

Follow the tunnel to another underground room. On one of the panels you'll find a guy dressed as a fruit bat. He'll tell you about the bones of a great beast. Keep going left until you come to a big, gold shark statue.

Climb to the top and then jump down on the left side. You'll find an Old Bone on the floor that you can pick up. Climb back up the shark statue and jump from platform to platform until you land on a tall stone pillar with sharp spikes on one side. Wait for the floating platform to reach you, then jump on that. It will take you

to another tunnel. This one leads to a room with carvings on the walls that show you the three ingredients for the Medicine Man's Potion: the Old Bone, the Carbonated Coconut Milk, and the Key Ingredient. Keep going left to get the Key Ingredient. Then shimmy up the vine to leave the temple.

TAMING THE BEAST

Now that you have the three ingredients for the Potion, go see the Medicine Man again. Talk to him and he will make the Potion for you. Head to Booga Bay and feed a coconut and the Potion to the Great Booga. The Potion will put the shark to sleep. Swim to the next island where you will find the long-lost Professor Hammerhead as well as the missing boy! Lead them both back to shore to earn your Island Medallion.

FYI If you take a look around Professor Hammerhead's Island, you'll see Wilson, the volleyball from the Tom Hanks movie *Cast Away.*

SHARK TOOTH MEDALLION

TIME TANGLED ISLAND

DIFFICULTY: EASY

SYNOPSIS: THE FUTURE IS IN DANGER, AND ONLY YOU CAN SAVE IT! ON THIS ISLAND, YOU CAN TRAVEL BACK IN TIME TO ELEVEN EXCITING PERIODS IN HISTORY. YOU'LL HAVE TO PERFORM A TASK IN EACH PLACE IN ORDER TO SAVE THE FUTURE. ALONG THE WAY, YOU'LL MEET SOME OF HISTORY'S MOST FASCINATING FIGURES.

FIRST STOP: MAIN STREET

Head right after you step onshore and you'll come to the Party Time Tower, a multi-player room. If you keep going, you'll come to Pendulum's Lab. Talk to the woman wearing glasses outside, and she'll tell you that the future is in peril. Follow her inside. If you agree to help, you will get a Mission Printout for your Inventory.

Inside the lab you'll find the Future Machine. A scientist will tell you that you can use it if you power it up. That's pretty easy—just jump down to the ground floor and push in the plug. Then go back up to the machine and enter through the door.

You'll be transported to a scary-looking future of gray skies and ruined buildings. Walk left to meet your white-haired future self. Your future self will give you a Time Device, which looks like a gold pocket watch. An icon of the device will appear on the bottom left of your screen; click on it any time you want to travel through time.

USING THE TIME DEVICE

When you open the watch you'll see that instead of numbers, there are people wearing clothes from different eras in time. Click on the Poptropican you want to visit and then click on the knob on the left of the Time Device to go that time period.

It doesn't matter where you start. Wherever you end up, you'll find a person who will tell you about an object they need. If you look around that time period, you will find an object—but not the right one. It's like the objects got tangled up in time! By now you've probably figured out what you need to do: Find the missing objects and return them to the right time periods. Once you return an object, the words *Time Period Repaired* will appear on your screen.

TIP:
Everywhere you go, you'll see small, round symbols floating in different spots. This is the Fact Monster, the official mascot of factmonster.com. Click on him to get more information about the time period you're in.

HINT:
You may have an easier time completing each task if you begin at the top left and travel counterclockwise around the circle.

0328 BC: ANCIENT GREECE

Click on the man with the golden helmet to get here. If you talk to the temple guards, they'll tell you that a Golden Vase is missing from the Treasury. Once you get the Golden Vase (from another time period), you can talk to the Oracle. She will give you advice that can help you find one of the items you need. If you climb to the top of the Treasury, you'll find the Phonograph, one of the missing items.

0831 BC: VIKINGS

Click on the man in the red beard and metal helmet to get here. You'll talk to some Vikings who are stranded on an island, waiting out a storm. Their leader will tell you they need Thor's Hammer. If you explore the island, you'll find a cave blocked by rocks on top of a mountain. There's an object inside the cave—the Golden Vase—but you won't be able to get to it now. First, you'll have to find some way to get past the rocks.

SECRET:

After you deliver the Notebook to Leonardo da Vinci, he'll give you a Glider. Climb up to the top of the mountain on the Vikings' island and put on the Glider. Then fly right to the next tall rock. There you'll find a Viking Suit that you can add to your Inventory.

32

1387 AD: THE MALI EMPIRE

Click on the woman in the pink turban to get here. Climb up the buildings until you meet a trader. He's missing his Salt Rocks. You'll need to get inside the Timbuktu Inn to find the object hidden here. Once inside, you'll meet another trader who has rare documents. Help him piece together a painting, and he'll give you the Declaration of Independence.

IT'S A PORTRAIT OF THE GREAT KING MANSA MUSA! THIS IS WONDERFUL!

TIP:
Jumping over the snakes is the best way to get past them.

ΓΝΩΘΙ ΣΕΑΥΤΟΝ

1516 AD: DA VINCI'S WORKSHOP

Click on the man with the gray beard and brown hat to get here. Follow the signs to Leo's Workshop, where you can meet legendary inventor and painter Leonardo da Vinci. He's missing his Notebook full of ideas for his inventions. Explore the platforms, ropes, and pulleys outside the workshop, and you'll discover the Peace Medal.

THERE'S A STRANGE OBJECT HANGING FROM THE BOTTOM OF THE DECK!

← Leo's workshop

1519 AD: AZTEC EMPIRE

Click on the man with the blue headdress to get here. You'll find yourself in a land of majestic stone pyramids. Climb up the second pyramid, and an Aztec warrior will tell you a Sun Stone Piece is missing from the elaborate sun stone. Climb up the third pyramid, and you'll meet an old warrior who will give you a Warrior Mask. Put it on and talk to some of the warriors on the ground. One of them will give you the Goggles.

FIND OUT WHAT HAPPENED TO THE SUN STONE!

1593 AD: GREAT WALL OF CHINA

Click on the man with the mustache and the gray helmet to get here. Climb the wall and look for a guard wearing armor. He'll tell you he needs a Stone Bowl so he can send smoke signals and communicate with other guards along the wall. Explore the wall and you will find a man wearing an Amulet shaped like a Hammer—Thor's Hammer, to be exact. Beat him in a memory game and he will give it to you.

HINT:

When you land, head right, moving up and down until you find a Gunpowder Barrel on a grassy hill. You'll find that you can put it in your Inventory. Hmm. This might be just what you need to blast your way into the mountain cave in the time of the Vikings.

1776 AD: GRAFF HOUSE

Click on the man in the black tricornered hat to get here. You'll find yourself smack in the middle of the American Revolution in Philadelphia, Pennsylvania. Inside the Graff House, Thomas Jefferson is working on the Declaration of Independence. Talk to him and he'll tell you it's missing. Explore the rooftops on this street to find the Salt Rocks.

I AM CAPTAIN MERIWETHER LEWIS.

I AM THOMAS JEFFERSON.

1805 AD: LEWIS AND CLARK

Click on the man in the beaver hat to get here. You'll meet famed explorers Lewis and Clark and their guide, Sacagawea. Lewis will tell you they can't go any farther without a Peace Medal. If you climb the tree, you'll see a bear popping out of the trunk on top with one of the missing objects on his head: the Stone Bowl.

1877 AD: EDISON'S WORKSHOP

Click on the clean-shaven man with short brown hair to enter here. Things are busy in the workshop of inventor Thomas Edison. One of his assistants will tell you that one of Edison's greatest inventions, the Phonograph, is missing. The Sun Stone Piece can be found on the workshop's roof, but how will you get all the way up there?

IT'S AN INVENTION OF MINE THAT RECORDS AND PLAYS SOUNDS.

HINT:
Try riding the wheeled vehicle, an early automobile, and see where it takes you.

1882 AD: THE STATUE OF LIBERTY

Click on the hatless man with the brown mustache and beard to get here. You'll end up in France, where the Statue of Liberty is under construction. If you go inside the studio of Gaget, Gauthier et Cie, you'll meet the sculptor, who is missing the Statuette of Liberty—a small model upon which the giant statue is based. If you climb the scaffolding outside, you will find a Notebook.

1953: MOUNT EVEREST

Click on the man in the blue hood to get here. Here you'll meet Edmund Hillary, one of the first explorers to reach the top of this frozen peak. You'll have to climb . . . and climb . . . and climb to get to him. Hillary will tell you he's missing his Goggles and can't reach the top without them. Climb as high as you can to find the Statuette of Liberty.

BACK TO THE FUTURE

Once you have returned all of the items, use your Time Device to go back to the lab. Use the Future Machine once more (you'll have to power it up again) to travel to the future. If you've done things right, you'll find a bright and sunny future waiting for you. Explore until you find your future self again. Once you find him or her, they will give an Island Medallion to you.

TAKE THIS GOLD MEDALLION. YOU'VE EARNED IT!

TIME TWISTED MEDALLION

24 CARROT ISLAND

DIFFICULTY: EASY
SYNOPSIS: THE RESIDENTS OF THIS ISLAND ARE GOING THROUGH SOME HARD TIMES. ONCE HOME TO THRIVING CARROT FARMS, THE CARROTS HAVE ALL DISAPPEARED. THE CARROT FACTORY IS CLOSED, IT'S HARD TO FIND JOBS, AND SOME POPTROPICANS HAVE GONE MISSING UNDER MYSTERIOUS CIRCUMSTANCES. ONCE YOU START INVESTIGATING, YOU'LL DISCOVER A SINISTER VILLAIN IS BEHIND THE ISLAND'S TROUBLES. ARE YOU CLEVER ENOUGH TO STOP THIS RABBITY ROGUE?

FIRST STOP: MAIN STREET

When you land on this Island, it's easy to see that something's wrong. The buildings are run-down, the Island sign is falling apart, and the mayor is in tears. Talk to him (the guy in the top hat) and he'll tell you about the missing carrots.

You'll see a sign for the Carrot Farm on your left, but explore Main Street first before you head there. Your first stop is the Carrot King Diner. Inside you'll meet a waitress holding a pitcher of milk. You'll also see a bulletin board with posters of four missing Poptropicans. Just for fun, fill up a cup with an Ice Cold Drink in the color of your choice. Click *Drink* and your hair color will change!

Leave the café for now and keep heading right. You'll pass the Cinema, which is closed for business, but you'll find a busy multiplayer room inside. Next is Charlie's Carrot Surplus Co. Inside, Charlie will tell you about her lost cat. If you find it, she'll give you a free crowbar. Ask her, and she'll let you know that she last saw her cat by the old farm house.

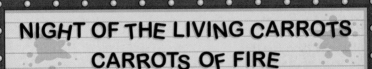

NIGHT OF THE LIVING CARROTS
CARROTS OF FIRE

Did You Know?:
The movies playing in the Cinema are *Night of the Living Carrots* and *Carrots of Fire*. These titles are parodies of two classic films, *Night of the Living Dead* and *Chariots of Fire*.

Remember that sign you saw for the Carrot Farm? Now it's time to head there to look for the cat. The old farm house is boarded up, so you'll have to find another way to enter. Jump up to the roof to find the way in.

On the first floor, you'll find a glass bowl that you can add to your Inventory. If you explore the second floor, you'll find the cat if you check carefully. No matter how hard you try, you won't be able to catch the cat. If only you had some way to lure it to you . . . wait a second. Didn't that waitress have a pitcher of milk?

Go back to the diner and talk to the waitress. She'll fill your glass bowl with milk for you. Go back to the old farm house. When you enter, you'll automatically put the bowl on the floor. Go upstairs and find the cat again. If you get the cat downstairs, it will drink the milk and then follow you wherever you go.

HINT:
To get the cat downstairs, move slowly and always stay a few steps behind it.

Now head back to Main Street and return the cat to Charlie. She'll give you a crowbar in return. You've helped Charlie, which is great. But the Island is still in trouble. You need to find out why all the carrots are disappearing. That means you need to go to the Carrot Factory.

THANK YOU! I CAN'T AFFORD TO GIVE YOU MUCH, BUT MAYBE YOU COULD USE THIS CROWBAR.

THE CARROT FACTORY

The Factory appears to be closed, and there are lots of signs telling you to stay away. If you want to get inside, you'll have to find a way in. If you jump up to the top of the roof, you'll find a Vent Blueprint. It's a map of the mazelike system of vents inside the Factory. Start looking around for a pipe that can get you inside the Factory. When you find it, a white hand symbol will appear. Click on it to use your crowbar to open the covering of the pipe.

You're in! Walk along the pipe and you'll find the Carrot Transporter. You can use this to exit the Factory if you need to. Keep working your way up. Soon you'll find an entrance into the main part of the Factory.

TIP:

You'll have to get across a row of valves that open and shut. Take them one at a time and move as quickly as you can when each valve shuts so you can get across.

THE MASTER ENGINE

In this room you'll find the Master Engine's control panel. Move the three levers until each light turns green. The Master Engine will turn on, and the room will light up. Now start looking for a way into the vents.

HINT:
When you see the giant mechanical arm, jump on it.

THE VENTS AND THE FREEZER

Getting through the vent system is a lot like getting through a maze. If you get stuck, click on the map icon on the lower left hand corner of the screen and use the Vent Blueprint to help you. In this section of the vents you'll find the Wire Cutters, which you'll need soon. After you grab them, move down and to the right and look for another grate in the vent.

Go through this hole and you'll be zapped by a security robot who'll transport you into the Freezer. Luckily, you have the Wire Cutters, which you can use to cut the wires on the Security System. Now you can keep exploring safely. Move right until you see another grate you can get through.

TIP:
To save time and trouble, make sure you have the Wire Cutters before you encounter the security robot.

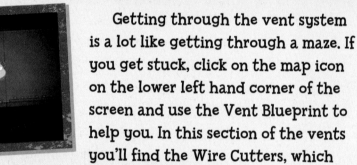

42

THE PACKING ROOM AND
THE PRINTING ROOM

Go through the grate and you'll find yourself in the Packing Room, where carrots are being packed into crates. You've found the missing carrots! But where are they going, and who is packing them?

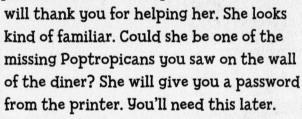

Run past the falling crates until you get to the other side. Then jump down to the factory floor and head left. You'll see a printer—you can find some answers there. Before you can use it, a girl wearing a helmet that looks like rabbit ears will try to stop you. Talk to her to distract her. Then press the button on top of her helmet. She will thank you for helping her. She looks kind of familiar. Could she be one of the missing Poptropicans you saw on the wall of the diner? She will give you a password from the printer. You'll need this later.

THANK YOU! NOW BE CAREFUL. IF YOU'RE SEEN WITHOUT RABBOT EARS DR. HARE WILL CATCH YOU!

Go back through the grate into the vent system and look for another grate. If you end up back in the Packing Room, you'll meet more people wearing bunny ear helmets. Use the same tactic to turn off their helmets. Keep going until you find a door with a sign that says Authorized Bunny Drones Only.

You're not an Authorized Bunny Drone, so a trap door will open up beneath you. You'll land on a conveyor belt in a new factory room. Travel across the conveyor belt, being careful to avoid being squished by the carrot presses or splashed with hot rabbit juice. At the end of the belt, jump up and look for Drone Ears. Put it on and head for the nearest exit. Now you look like an Authorized Bunny Drone!

Now you can go through the door that says Authorized Bunny Drones Only. Inside, you'll find . . . Dr. Hare, a super-villain wearing a pink bunny suit and green goggles. He thinks you're one of his drones and asks you to start the launch sequence for his rabbit-shaped spaceship. You're finally starting to put the pieces of the mystery together. It looks like Dr. Hare took all the carrots and turned them into rocket fuel!

Head for the control panel and distract the drone guarding it. Then enter the password you got before. The computer will ask you for a launch code. You'll find one on a note on the computer—make sure you type it in exactly.

"DR. HARE IS MY FAVORITE CHARACTER IN POPTROPICA. HE'S LIKE THE TRADITIONAL EVIL MAD SCIENTIST."
—HADES, A POPTROPICA CREATOR

Now you're in control of Dr. Hare's spaceship! Use the joystick to control it as it moves through space. In a normal video game, you'd want to avoid obstacles like asteroids. But you don't want Dr. Hare to escape, do you? Crash the spaceship into the asteroids until Dr. Hare goes spiraling off into space.

A HAPPY ENDING

Shimmy up the nearest rope to get out of the factory. Now that Dr. Hare is gone, the Island looks a lot better. Find the mayor on Main Street and he'll give you your Island Medallion.

THE ORIGINS OF DR. HARE

HE STEALS FROM CARROT-LOVING ISLANDERS. HE TURNS INNOCENT POPTROPICANS INTO DRONES. HE'S THE EPITOME OF AN EVIL VILLAIN . . . IN A PINK BUNNY SUIT. JUST WHO IS DR. HARE?

THIS CHARACTER STEMS FROM THE IMAGINATION OF A POPTROPICA CREATOR (AKA. SHARK BOY). WHEN HE WAS IN COLLEGE, SHARK BOY CREATED A COMIC BOOK ABOUT A HERO NAMED CARROT TEEN, A RADIOACTIVE CARROT. THE BEST NEMESIS FOR A CARROT IS A RABBIT, OF COURSE. AND THAT'S HOW DR. HARE WAS BORN.

SUPER POWER ISLAND

DIFFICULTY: MEDIUM

SYNOPSIS: HAVE YOU EVER WANTED TO FLY THROUGH THE AIR AND FIGHT BAD GUYS, JUST LIKE A REAL SUPERHERO? THAT'S EXACTLY WHAT YOU CAN DO ON THIS ISLAND. ONCE YOU GET SUITED UP IN YOUR COSTUME, YOU CAN CHASE SIX VILLAINS WHO'VE ESCAPED FROM PRISON. THERE'S ONLY ONE CATCH—THEY'VE GOT CRAZY POWERS AFTER BEING EXPOSED TO A RADIOACTIVE METEOR. DO YOU HAVE WHAT IT TAKES TO PUT THEM BEHIND BARS AGAIN?

FIRST STOP: MAIN STREET

This street looks like a pleasant street you'd find in most cities—except the citizens you meet are freaking out. There was a break at the prison, and everyone's in danger. You can go left and explore the prison now, if you like, but you won't get very far unless you make a few stops first. Head right and go into the Comic Shop.

Talk to Ned Noodlehead, the superhero-obsessed owner of the shop. Talk to him and he'll give you *The Superhero's Handbook*, which he wrote himself. Take a minute to read it. Besides being funny, it contains some good advice for catching bad guys.

THE SUPERHERO'S HANDBOOK

written and illustrated by NED NOODLEHEAD

Then walk next door into the
Masks & Capes shop. The owner
will give you a Super Hero ID Card.
Click on the costumes in the shop
to create your custom hero look.
You can mix a mask from one costume with a cape
from another. Your final look is up to you. Now that
you're all suited up, you're almost ready to start

fighting crime. You just need a
few more things first. It's time to
head to the Prison.

SUPER HERO IDENTIFICATION CARD

ID # - 1312409012

STATUS:
Active

SUPER HERO

VILLAINS DEFEATED

THE PRISON

Go left to get to the Prison—you'll have to swim there,
but it's not far. Climb onshore and you'll see how the

prisoners escaped—there's a huge
meteor sticking out of the broken prison
wall. Talk to the warden and he'll give
you some Super Villain Files. When you
capture a villain, you'll get a sticker
in the book to show you've succeeded.
Speak to the woman in glasses and she'll

tell you that the prisoners have been mutated by radiation.
She gives you Anti-Power Handcuffs so you can bring the
villains back to the prison after you catch them.

You're finally ready to start rounding up the escaped
evildoers. Time to head Down Town!

CAPTURE COPY CAT

On your way Down Town you'll pass by a telephone booth and *The Daily Paper*, a multi-player room. Keep going until you reach the Down Town area. The first building you'll see is the Bank. A police officer will tell you that the bank has been robbed by Copy Cat, and they can't catch her.

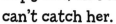

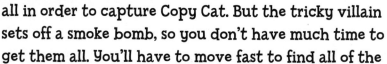

If you enter the bank and walk left, you'll find Copy Cat. She will make several copies of herself and they'll all run away and hide in the bank. You'll have to catch them all in order to capture Copy Cat. But the tricky villain sets off a smoke bomb, so you don't have much time to get them all. You'll have to move fast to find all of the copies, which are on the second floor as well. Take the elevator to reach the second floor. You'll also find some copies on the first floor on top of the light fixtures.

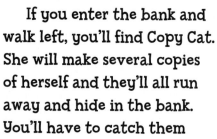

Each time you catch a villain, you'll make the front page of the paper and go back to the Prison to put him or her behind bars. Check your Super Villain Files, and you'll see her sticker there. That's one down, five to go!

TIP:
Before you talk to Copy Cat, go to the elevator and push the button so it comes down to the first floor. That will save time so you can catch all of the copies before the smoke fills the Bank.

SUBDUE SPEEDING SPIKE

Head right past the Bank and go down into the Subway Station to find Speeding Spike, another escaped villain. You'll find him inside the subway train—he's the dude with green hair holding a bag of money. He'll try to hit you with that bag, so you've got to keep jumping over him to avoid the blows. You need to let him chase you into the first subway car, where he'll slip on a puddle. Then walk right up to him and place the handcuffs on him.

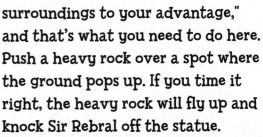

SIR REBRAL ROCKS

Leave the subway and walk past the Subway Station to the City Park. Sir Rebral is standing on top of a broken statue. He's wearing weird green glasses and using the power of his mind to toss heavy rocks around like they're beach balls. First, you've got to avoid getting hit by the rocks. If you jump to avoid them, they'll hit Sir Rebral instead and he'll get angry.

Pieces of the ground will start to break underneath your feet. *The Superhero Handbook* advises you to "use your surroundings to your advantage," and that's what you need to do here. Push a heavy rock over a spot where the ground pops up. If you time it right, the heavy rock will fly up and knock Sir Rebral off the statue.

SURF THE SEWERS

Fighting crime can sometimes be a dirty business. To catch Ratman, you'll need to head down to the stinky sewers. Get there by going into the public restroom in the park. Then head down the hole next to the toilet.

Go down to the first wheel you see and click on it. That will cause the water level to drop so you can explore the bottom of the sewer. As the water sinks, you'll see a platform with a door on the wall behind it. You can try to jump up to it, but it's too high. Find another wheel and the wall will rise. Now jump to the platform and enter the door.

You'll see Ratman surrounded by flies, standing on a pipe next to a bag of money. Climb up the pipes, jumping over the rats that will try to attack you. When you reach the red wheel, click on it. A strong spray of water will knock Ratman to his feet. Hurry over to his pipe to capture him before his flies bite you.

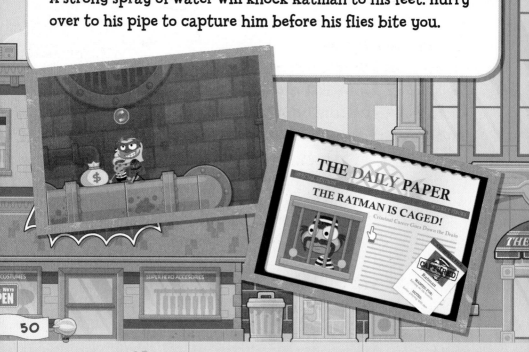

THE DAILY PAPER

THE RATMAN IS CAGED!

Criminal Career Goes Down the Drain

CATCH CRUSHER

By now you could probably use a shower, but you've got to finish cleaning up the city first. Go right past the City Park and enter the Junkyard. You'll find Crusher standing on top of a heap of scrap metal. There's a refrigerator over his head, dangling from a magnet on the end of the arm of a crane. He'll start hurling heavy barrels at you using his superstrength.

Ned Noodlehead told you to "use your brain," and that's just what you'll need to do to take down this muscled madman. The key to defeating Crusher is using the power of the magnet. If you can get into the crane, you can deactivate the magnet. The refrigerator will fall on his head—but he's got superstrength, remember? Angry, Crusher will toss it at you. What can you do now?

Time to use the magnet again. If you activate it, the metal underneath Crusher will rise up toward the magnet—and Crusher will be crushed by the arm of the crane. Now *that's* using your noodle!

I REALLY ENJOYED ANIMATING CRUSHER. IT WAS FUN TO HAVE CRUSHER SHAKING THE WORLD.—DR. HARE, A POPTROPICA CREATOR

TAKE TO THE SKIES

The very last villain, Betty Jetty, has the power of flight. There's no way you can battle her unless you can fly, too. That's why you need to be sure to walk past the telephone booth on Main Street one more time. The phone will ring, and you'll be given the power of flight. There'll be a blue icon in the left corner of your screen. Click on it whenever you want to fly.

Go Down Town and fly to the top of the Skyscraper. That's where you'll spot a villain with spiky pink hair—Betty Jetty. She'll cry, "Catch me if you can!" and then take off.

TELEPHONE
Ringing

CATCH ME IF YOU CAN!

WHACK!

IT'S GOING TO TAKE MORE THAN THAT TO STOP ME! BWAAH HA HA!!!

SUPERHERO ACCESORIES

Fly after her. She'll hurl green energy balls at you, which you have to avoid. Keep at it until you're close enough to bump into her. You and Betty Jetty will land on top of a building, where she will tell you that you haven't won yet. Out of the blue, a secret sidekick will appear and knock her down. Betty Jetty is captured—and she's the last escaped villain!

SECRET:

After you get the power of flight, go right up on top of *The Daily Paper* building. You'll meet a mysterious white-haired hero who will tell you, "With great power comes great responsibility." He's actually a combination of several heroes.

YOUR TRUSTY SIDEKICK HAS ARRIVED!

A HOT DOG FOR A HERO

Talk to the Warden and he'll tell you that he gave the Island Medallion to the real hero of the day—Ned Noodlehead, your secret sidekick. Luckily, Ned is willing to trade the Medallion to you if you get him a hot dog from the vendor in the park.

SO I'D BE WILLING TO TRADE THIS MEDALLION FOR A GOOD HOT DOG!

SPY ISLAND

DIFFICULTY: MEDIUM

SYNOPSIS: WHEN YOU LAND ON THIS ISLAND, YOU TAKE ON A WHOLE NEW IDENTITY: YOU'RE A SECRET AGENT. YOU'LL GET EQUIPPED WITH SOME COOL SPY GEAR AND THEN GIVEN A MISSION: FIND AND RESCUE THREE TOP SPIES WHO'VE BEEN CAPTURED BY B.A.D., THE BALD AND DANGEROUS ORGANIZATION. IT WON'T BE EASY, BECAUSE B.A.D.'S AGENTS ARE EVERYWHERE, AND THEY'LL TRY TO STOP YOU EVERY CHANCE THEY GET.

FIRST STOP: MAIN STREET

THE BALD AND DANGEROUS ORGANIZATION. THEY'RE UP TO SOMETHING BAD, AND WE'VE GOT TO STOP IT!

When you land, the first person you meet will tell you that Director D. is waiting for you inside Headquarters. That's the first building on your right. Go inside and jump to the top floor where you'll find Director D., a smooth-looking guy in a white tuxedo. Talk to him and he'll tell you that B.A.D. has captured the agency's three top spies. He'll give you a decoder kit. Talk to him one more time, and he'll tell you that one of the spies was last seen on the Docks.

Before you head there, leave Headquarters and go next

door to Spyglass Eyewear. If you climb the ladder, you see it takes you to a door, but you can't get in. Go through the front door and pick up a pair of eyeglasses from one of the displays. Head left and talk to Dr. Spyglass, the eye doctor.

Ask for an eye exam. If you do it correctly, he'll recognize that you're a secret agent and ask you to meet him upstairs.

HINT:

Dr. Spyglass will know he can trust you only if you give him *opposite* answers on the exam.

Go outside and climb up to the door again. This time, it will open. Dr. Spyglass will give you his latest invention, the Chameleon Suit. When you put it on, you will blend into your surroundings.

RESCUE THE FIRST AGENT

Now you're ready to head to the Docks. Head left past Headquarters. You'll pass the Hair Club, a multi-player room. You'll see a mysterious red laser shoot down from the sky, completely removing all the hair from the head of an unsuspecting woman. Could this also be the work of B.A.D.?

When you get to the Docks, talk to the spy you find hiding in a garbage can. He'll give you a Secret Message. Use your decoder to figure out what it says. The message will tell you where you need to go to find the first missing spy: the roof.

Go to the first building and make your way up. The place is crawling with B.A.D. guards. Make sure you're wearing your Chameleon Suit. Stand completely still when a guard approaches, and you won't be seen.

Jump from the first rooftop to the next to find an entrance to the warehouse. Snarling dogs will try to stop you—it's a good thing you're still wearing your Chameleon Suit. Search until you find the first kidnapped spy, who's tied up with rope. Click on him to set him free, and he'll give you the Laser Pen, which can cut through metal.

He'll also give you a Satellite Clue. It won't make sense to you yet, but it's good that you have it. Now you're done with the Docks, so head back to Main Street.

I'LL TAKE CARE OF THE DOOR GUARD!

GO UNDERCOVER IN THE B.A.D. BISTRO

Walk down Main Street until you get to Balding Avenue. Look for the B.A.D. Bistro, a notorious bad guy hangout. You might be able to learn something useful here, so go to the kitchen and ask the chef for a job. If you pass his test, you'll get a Chef Hat you can wear. Put it on and talk to some of the B.A.D. agents who are dining.

A guy with a mustache will ask you to take his glass. When you do that, you'll see it has his Fingerprint on it. This could be useful.

You've got to get out of the restaurant quickly before the B.A.D. guys stop you. If you pass by the diners, you won't be able to get out. You'll have to find a way to get to the front door without them seeing you.

HINT:
To safely get to the door, go back to the kitchen and head up!

I THINK THIS LETTER CONTAINS A HIDDEN MESSAGE, BUT I CAN'T DECODE IT.

Run to the right and you'll see a fellow spy in the bushes wearing camouflage. Talk to him and he'll tell you he has a secret letter, but he can't decode it. He'll give it to you. Your decoder won't work on this—you'll have to move the paper in the folder until one line of letters appears in the shadow. The message you see is intriguing: "Don't trust Director D."

Armed with that information, keep heading right until you reach Toupée Terrace. Try to walk to the door, and one of the security lights will zap you. You need to investigate this house, so make your way to the roof, timing your movements to avoid the lights. You'll come to a window blocked by metal bars. It's a good thing you have the Laser Pen! Climb into the attic and you'll find the second kidnapped agent.

Click on him to untie him. He'll give you the Grappling Bowtie and another Satellite Clue.

I HAVE SOMETHING THAT WILL HELP YOU ON YOUR MISSION.

THE AMAZING GRAPPLING BOWTIE

NINE OUT OF TEN POPTROPICANS AGREE: THE GRAPPLING BOWTIE IS ONE OF THE COOLEST ITEMS YOU CAN GET. YOU CAN USE IT TO SWING FROM BUILDING TO BUILDING LIKE SPIDER-MAN, AND YOU CONTROL WHERE YOU GO. WHILE THIS ITEM IS EXTRA FUN FOR POPTROPICANS, IT WAS EXTRA CHALLENGING FOR THE GAME DEVELOPERS TO CREATE.

"THE CHARACTERS HAD NEVER MOVED IN EXACTLY THAT WAY BEFORE," EXPLAINS DR. HARE, A POPTROPICA CREATOR. "IT REQUIRED SOME CLEVER REPURPOSING OF THE PLATFORM AND CHARACTER CODE."

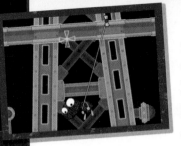

Go back to Balding Avenue and stand on the wall next to the spy in camouflage. Use your Grappling Bowtie to swing from building to building. Control it by clicking on the bowtie icon on the bottom left of your screen, then click where you want to throw it.

You'll want to go as high as you can get. It takes some practice, so keep trying until you get the hang of it. You're looking for the roof of the Greenhouse, which is made of glass. Once you get inside, look around until you find the third agent, a woman in a black dress. She's trapped in a metal cage, but your Laser Pen won't work on these bars. You'll need to find another way to get through them.

Explore and you'll find the Cherry Bomb Tree. Click on the Cherry Bomb, and it will fall off the tree. If you push it up to the cage, it will explode and the bars will blow open. The grateful spy will give you Ultra Vision Goggles, which allow you to see invisible lasers, and another Satellite Clue.

TIP:
There are lots of B.A.D. agents on the rooftops. You might want to put on your Chameleon Suit so you can avoid them.

WOW, I'M GLAD I'M STILL IN ONE PIECE!

Cherry Bomb Tree

HINT:
The lily pad-like plants on the floor are capable of shooting large objects into the air.

THE TRUTH ABOUT DIRECTOR D.

You may have rescued the three missing agents, but your mission isn't over. You need to figure out who's behind the missing agents as well as the missing hair. Head right until you come to the B.A.D. Control Center.

The place is guarded by lasers, so it's a good thing you're wearing your special Goggles. The lasers flash on and off, so get through them one at a time. Then head up. You'll come to an entry door, but you can't enter unless it scans your Fingerprint. Luckily, you have a wine glass with the Fingerprint of a B.A.D. agent on it. That will get you inside.

Jump to a platform with computers on it and you'll quickly become trapped in a cage. Director D. shows up and sets you free. He asks you to get the Teleporter working. To

do that, you'll need to enter a code into the computer. Open up your items and click on all three Satellite Clues. Stack the clues on top of one another until the code is revealed. Then type the code into the transporter.

A beam shoots out of the machine, and Director D. jumps into it with a sinister, "Bwaa ha ha ha!" You're starting to suspect that something is up with him. Follow him into the transporter, and you'll find yourself in a room filled with strange machines.

Director D. will whip off his toupee and tell you his evil plan: to vaporize the hair of everyone in Poptropica! He disappears inside a space pod and sends his Mini-Bots after you. You'll need to destroy all of these one-armed floating robots. Luckily, there are several ports around the room that produce golden balls of energy. If you can get the robots to fly into the ports, they'll be destroyed. Use your Grappling Bowtie to help you move around the room.

Once you've taken care of the Mini-Bots, Director D. will get angry and start flying around in his space pod. The only way to destroy the pod is to get it to crash into the ceiling again and again. Director D. will give up. Your mission is complete!

To get your Island Medallion, go back to Headquarters and talk to the Secretary of the agency.

YOU'VE PUT AN END TO DIRECTOR D. AND HIS EVIL PLANS. OUR HAIR IS SAFE, THANKS TO YOU.

SECRET SECRETARY

SPY MEDALLION

CHOOSE YOUR OWN ADVENTURE®

NABOOTI  ISLAND

DIFFICULTY: MEDIUM

SYNOPSIS: THE CONTINENT OF AFRICA IS HOME TO ANCIENT TREASURES AND AMAZING NATURAL WONDERS. ON THIS ISLAND, YOU CAN BECOME A DARING ADVENTURER AND EXPLORE AFRICA WHILE YOU SEARCH FOR FIVE MISSING JEWELS. YOU'LL HAVE TO SOLVE PUZZLES, SURVIVE THE BLAZING DESERT AND MOUNTAIN PEAKS, AND EVEN PLAY A FEW DIRTY TRICKS TO GET WHAT YOU'RE AFTER. IN THE END, THE REWARD WILL BE MORE THAN YOU'VE EVER IMAGINED.

FIRST STOP: MAIN STREET

Jump off your blimp and enter this African village. For fun, head into the Choose Your Own Adventure building on the right to find out about an exciting book series. When you're ready to begin your Nabooti adventure, go left to the Nabooti African Museum. As you walk through, you'll notice some amazing art. Click on each piece to learn more about it.

THEY'VE BEEN LOST TO THE AGES. WE'VE ONLY MANAGED TO RECOVER TWO OF THEM.

On the ground floor you'll talk to a woman standing in front of the Nabooti Totem. She'll tell you that the statue came from the sky long ago. Ask her about the five missing jewels, and she'll say they were lost to the ages. The museum is looking for an adventurer to recover them. Are you up for the job?

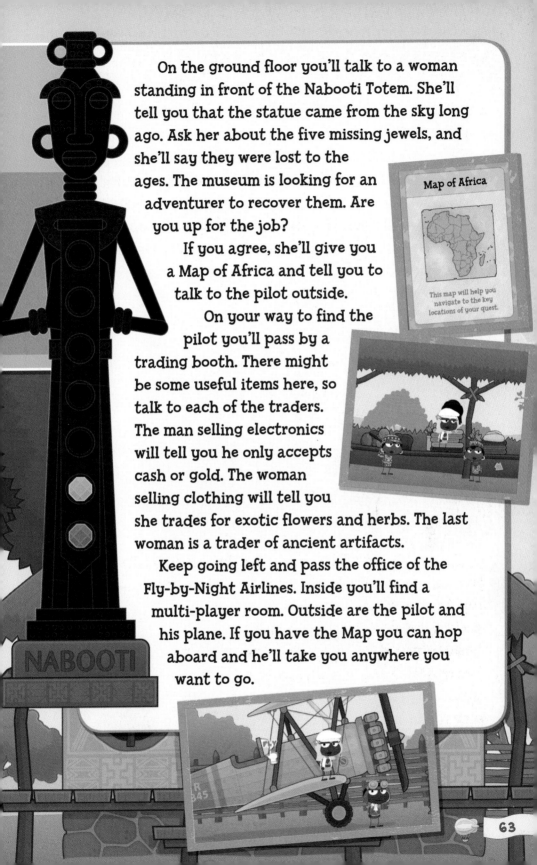

Map of Africa

This map will help you navigate to the key locations of your quest.

If you agree, she'll give you a Map of Africa and tell you to talk to the pilot outside.

On your way to find the pilot you'll pass by a trading booth. There might be some useful items here, so talk to each of the traders. The man selling electronics will tell you he only accepts cash or gold. The woman selling clothing will tell you she trades for exotic flowers and herbs. The last woman is a trader of ancient artifacts.

Keep going left and pass the office of the Fly-by-Night Airlines. Inside you'll find a multi-player room. Outside are the pilot and his plane. If you have the Map you can hop aboard and he'll take you anywhere you want to go.

NABOOTI

BLUE NILE FALLS

It doesn't matter where you go first, but Blue Nile Falls is a good place to start. Jump up the rocks to get to the top of the falls. While you're exploring, you should find the Egyptian Blue Lily. Keep looking around until you find a woman who needs help getting a chicken, a fox, and a basket of grain to the other side of a cliff. She gets across riding in a basket suspended by ropes and pulleys. You can only fit one thing in the basket at a time. If you leave the chicken and the grain together on one side, the chicken will eat the grain. If you leave the fox and the chicken together, the fox will eat the chicken.

If you succeed, the woman will tell you that there is

HINT: This challenge is based on an old riddle with a trick to it: You can always move an item back to the right side of the cliff to even things out.

a secret cave hidden by a big bush near the waterfall. Enter the cave and watch out for the falling stalactites. You'll find the Purple Jewel inside. Now head back to your plane.

TIME TO TRADE

Remember the trader who accepts exotic flowers and herbs? Go back to Nabooti Island and talk to her. She will trade you a Desert Turban for the Egyptian Blue Lily. You'll need the turban later.

WOULD YOU BE WILLING TO TRADE THAT EGYPTIAN BLUE LILY FOR A FINE DESERT TURBAN?

FUEL   FUEL

THE KAYA FORESTS

This is a good time to head to the Kaya Forests. It's nighttime in this village of grass huts. You'll see animal skins drying on sticks. You won't find a jewel here yet—just a huge tortoise that seems to be asleep. Could there be a way to get it to move? Climb some trees and you'll find a Gold Nugget. Didn't that electronics trader say he accepted gold?

TRADING TIME AGAIN

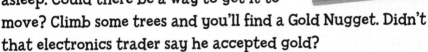

Fly back to Nabooti and talk to the electronics trader. He'll trade you the Gold Nugget for a Digital Camera. Hey, that would be a good thing to have on a safari, wouldn't it?

SAFARI SNAPSHOTS

Fly to the spot on the Map that reads *Safari* and talk to Big Zeke. Business has been slow, and he needs seven good photos of seven different animals from you. It's a good thing you have your Digital Camera. The only other thing you'll need to complete this challenge is a little bit of patience. Zeke will give you a Miner's Hard Hat as a reward. Hey, this might be a good time to check out the Diamond Mines!

Fly to the Diamond Mines and put on your Miner's Hard Hat. The mines are protected by an electric fence, so you'll have to find the switch to deactivate the fence before you can climb over it. You'll have to do this quickly before the electricity turns on again.

Look for a break in the barbed wire on top of the fence. That's the only way in.

Walk left and you'll see some platforms leading up to the mine shaft entrance. There are carts rolling down the platforms that you need to avoid. Wait for the first one to roll down before you start jumping up. Climb the platforms until you see the hole leading down into the mine shaft. Then jump in!

You won't be able to get very far—the tunnel is blocked by a wall of rocks. Luckily, there's a big barrel of explosives you can push up against the wall. Now you just need a way to light the fuse. Hmm. A few electric sparks might do the trick.

After you blast through the wall, push the mine cart forward and hop inside to begin a wild ride through the mine shaft. You'll have to jump over spikes and duck to avoid hitting your head. Keep going until you find a stash of diamonds. Click on them and you'll be able to examine them with a magnifying glass so you can identify the White Jewel from the Nabooti Totem.

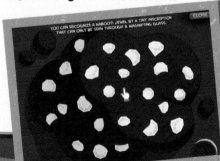

MOUNTAINS OF THE MOON

Whew! You've done a lot of adventuring so far, and you still need to find three jewels! This is a good time to go to the Mountains of the Moon. Start climbing up the mountain and you'll meet a woman who will tell you she can't reach the red fig just above you. Jump up and get it and you'll get to keep the Opuntia Fruit.

Keep heading up, avoiding goats as you climb (most of the time—sometimes they're useful for head-butting you to a higher level). As you get higher, the mountain will become very icy. That's a good sign. It means you're getting closer to an old man standing in front of a cave. Beat him in a game of Mancala and he'll let you inside. Don't worry if you don't know how to play—instructions and tips will appear as you go. It may take a few tries, but you'll get the hang of it.

LIFE IS LONELY UP HERE. BEAT ME IN MANCALA AND I'LL LET YOU ENTER THE CAVE!

Pick up the Cell Phone you find inside the cave. Then jump from rock to rock, avoiding falling icicles, until you find the Red Jewel.

THE SECRET OF THE CELL PHONE

CURIOUS POPTROPICANS HAVE BEEN SURPRISED TO FIND THAT EXCITING THINGS HAPPEN WHEN THEY DIAL CERTAIN NUMBERS ON THE CELL PHONE. DIAL 911, AND A POLICEMAN'S CAP WILL APPEAR ON YOUR HEAD. DIALING 411 WILL CALL UP A GLASS CASE HOLDING A BRAIN YOU CAN WEAR AS A HAT. TRY 1225 (DECEMBER 25, GET IT?) AND YOU'LL GET A SANTA HAT. OR TRY 1337 IF YOU WANT TO LOOK LIKE A NERD.

Head north to Giza, where you'll find an archaeological team digging outside the ancient statue of the Sphinx, a mythical creature with the body of a lion and the head of a human. That seems like a good hiding place for a missing jewel, doesn't it? You won't be able to get past the workers to get inside, though. But if you put on your Desert Turban and talk to the first worker, he'll think you're there to help and give you a Shovel. If you look closely at the handle, you'll see a phone number there.

Walk right and talk to the archaeologist. He's not much help. You really need to get into the Sphinx—maybe you can distract him somehow. Get your Cell Phone from your items and dial the number on the Shovel. That will do the trick. Before you leave the area, click on the bag you see. Inside, you'll find the Moon Stone.

Climb up to the top of the Sphinx. You'll see a rod with a circle on top. The Moon Stone fits perfectly inside the circle! Put the stone in the circle and the moonlight will shine through the stone, opening the entrance to the Sphinx. Head inside and you'll find the next passage is blocked. To

open it, click on the stone tablet with the four rectangles on it. Click on the rectangles until all four of them line up horizontally and run across the stone tablet. The passageway will open for you.

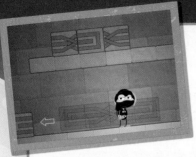

You'll come to four concrete blocks with carvings on them. You'll have to push them down to the next level in the correct order so that when you push them together, the design fits together like the pieces of a puzzle. (If you make a mistake, click on the *Reset* button to start again.) Once you complete the puzzle, a door will open above you. Push all four blocks to the left so you can jump up and reach the door.

Keep going up, and you will come to a room with two large statues in it. If you try to get to them, the floor will start to collapse underneath your feet. Be sure to jump on the right spot on each stone in the floor or else you will fall.

Once you're safe, take a look at the statues. Each figure is holding its hands open, palms up. Above each open hand is a stone weight with a number of dots on it. On each side of the statue is a lever that will release the weight and drop it onto the hand. When that happens, sand pours from the statue's mouth.

Pull the levers in the correct order and a sarcophagus will open up above you. Inside, you'll find the Blue Jewel.

HINT:
Look on the dots on each weight. They will tell you in which order you need to drop them.

TEMPTING THE TORTOISE

Only one jewel left to go! Look at the Map and try to remember where you haven't found a jewel yet. This is a good time to go back to the Kaya Forests.

Remember the sleeping tortoise? Check your items and see if there's anything in there that can get him moving. The Opuntia Fruit is just the thing. When the turtle gets up, you'll see the start of a hole in the dirt underneath him. Use your Shovel to dig and you'll find the Ebony Elephant.

After you find this artifact, two ghosts will appear. They tell you if you bring them a Fingo, they'll reward you.

THE FINAL TRADE

Go back to Nabooti and talk to the last trader to exchange the Ebony Elephant for a Fingo, an ancient protective talisman. Return to the forests and talk to the ghost wearing the Warrior Mask. He'll give you the Green Jewel as a reward.

THE TOTEM TAKES OFF

Return to the Nabooti African Museum. You'll have to place the jewels in the correct order on the Totem. The hints make this a pretty easy task. When you succeed, you'll learn the amazing secret of the Totem! The pleased woman in the museum will reward you with an Island Medallion.

CHOOSE YOUR OWN ADVENTURE · NABOOTI
MEDALLION

big NATE ISLAND

DIFFICULTY: EASY

SYNOPSIS: ON THIS ISLAND, YOU ENTER THE WORLD OF THE BIG NATE COMIC STRIP! YOU CAN PAL AROUND WITH NATE AND HIS FRIENDS AS YOU EXPLORE THEIR WORLD. BUT YOU'LL NEED TO DO MORE THAN JUST HANG OUT IN THE PLAYGROUND. EVERYBODY'S LOOKING FOR A TIME CAPSULE THAT'S SUPPOSED TO HOLD A TREASURE INSIDE. CAN YOU BE THE FIRST TO FIND IT?

FIRST STOP: MAIN STREET

Step onto this Island and Nate will be there to greet you. He'll tell you about the search for the Time Capsule. If you enter the first building, the Pop-In Shoppe, you'll meet Nate's dad. Read the bulletin board, and you'll find out that the treasure in the Time Capsule could save the school, which needs a lot of repair.

Jump up to the attic, and you'll find a piece of the Big Nate Comic. This could be useful.

Next door is the Klassic Komix shop. Explore here to read some Big Nate Comic strips. Talk to the guy in the Book Nook, and he'll tell you he's missing pieces of a

Big Nate Comic Book. (Hey, didn't you find one of those already?) If you collect all of the pieces he'll give you a reward.

Head outside and keep going right. You'll pass Cap'n Salty's seafood restaurant, a multi-player room. Go into the Say Cheese Photo Studio and talk to the School Picture Guy. He has some scuba equipment that he's willing to trade for an old photo.

That's about all you can do on Main Street right now. But before you leave, make sure to read one of the Lost Dog posters that are tacked up everywhere.

LOST DOG

HIS NAME IS SPITSY,
HE IS REDDISH-BROWN,
AND HE WILL DO **ANYTHING**
FOR PEANUT BUTTER CRACKERS!

HAVE YOU SEEN HIM??

TIME FOR SCHOOL

When you get to the school, you'll see that the place is a wreck. Everyone you talk to seems to be looking for the Time Capsule. Head upstairs and you'll find one of the comic strip pieces on top of a speaker. You'll also see a locker overflowing with stuff, but you won't be able to open it without a combination.

Go inside the Science Lab and look for another comic piece there. If you talk to Francis, he'll warn you that the chemicals in the lab are dangerous. If you're anything like Nate, you'll click on them, anyway. Mix the chemicals in the beaker, turn up the heat, and if you create a mixture that's exactly the right shade of green, you'll get a Stink Bomb.

HINT:
Don't put in too much blue or too much yellow.
The green mixture needs to be just right!

73

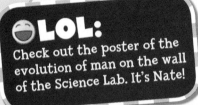

You're probably thinking that the Time Capsule might be inside the school somewhere. That's not a bad thought. The only door you can't get in is marked *Detention*. You'll have to figure out a way to get in there later.

Leave the school and climb up the scaffolding to find another comic book piece. You can click on your items at any time and try to put the pieces together. At this point, you'll still need to find more.

RECESS

Head to the Playground and you'll find some girls hanging around during recess. You can try to talk to them, but they can't hear you—they're too busy talking to one another. You'll also spot Spitsy, the lost dog.

Climb up the jungle gym. If you go inside the Kids Clubhouse, you can play two games with Nate. Beat him at Table Football and you'll get *Big Nate's Practical Jokes*. Beat him at Go to Jail and you'll get a box of Peanut Butter Crackers.

If you've read the Lost Dog posters, you know that Spitsy likes Peanut Butter Crackers. Before you climb back down, explore the jungle gym some more—you'll find one more piece of the comic book. If you feed Spitsy the Peanut Butter Crackers, he'll dig into the ground. Not that exciting—but remember that Spitsy can do this. It may come in handy later.

PUFFIN POINT

Go right to Puffin Point and climb up the Lighthouse. You'll see an Old Photograph floating in the breeze. Keep climbing and you'll find the school's art teacher, Mr. Rosa, painting the view. You can look through the Telescope, but you won't see anything except ocean and sky. Jump up to the beacon on top of the Lighthouse. You won't be able to change the direction of this bright light without using something with a firm grip. Go all the way to the top to get the last missing piece of the comic strip. It's time to head back to Main Street!

TIP:
If you jump off the top of the Lighthouse, you can catch the Old Photograph on the way down.

A TRADE AND A REWARD

Run into the photo studio and trade the Old Photograph for the Scuba Gear. Then go into the comic book shop. Before you talk to the guy in the Book Nook, try to put the pieces together in the right order. If you succeed, you'll get a locker combination. You can use that to open the locker on the second floor of the school.

Give the missing pieces to the Book Nook guy and he'll give you a Pack of Stale Gum to thank you.

OYSTER
BEDS
↓

DETENTION

Go back to the school and use the combination to open the stuffed locker. When the dust clears, go to the pile of junk and pick up a School Blueprint. Examine it and you'll see there's a basement. Could that be where the Time Capsule is? And how do you get down there, anyway?

Looks like you'll have to get into the detention room somehow, and the best way to do that is to break the rules. Go to the No Gum Chewing sign and chew the gum you just got. Mrs. Godfrey will give you detention.

There doesn't seem to be a way into the basement—but you can't fully explore with Mrs. Godfrey around. Look in your items for a way to get rid of her. The Stink Bomb is just the thing! Use it and she'll flee to escape the smell.

Now you can get past her to the file cabinets. Click on them to reveal a secret entrance to the cellar.

Turn on the power switch so you can find your way around. You'll meet a grateful Time Capsule hunter who's been trapped down there. He'll tell you there's no Time Capsule to be found, but you might find something else you can use. Click on stuff you see until you pick up the Bell Clapper.

So it looks like the Time Capsule isn't in the school. Where else can you look? Might as well try to use that Scuba Gear you traded for.

Head back to Puffin Point and use your Scuba Gear to swim underwater. Find the Lobster Trap before your time ends and give it to the Fisherman. He'll give you his Jet Ski Keys and a Lobster as a reward. *What can you do with that?* you wonder. Well, a Lobster has a strong grip. It's just the thing you need to turn the handle of the Lighthouse beacon.

Climb the beacon and use the Lobster to swing the light around. The light will disturb a seagull hanging out by the bell on top of the school. When you climb back down, look through the Telescope one more time. This time, you'll see some seals hanging out on a rock—and there's a piece of paper underneath the rock. Could it be a clue?

WHAT'S THAT UNDER THE ROCK?

To get out to the rocks, you'll need to ride the Fisherman's jet ski. Nate will race you. You'll need to beat him to the rocks so you can explore. When you get there, you'll have to figure out how to move the rock so that you can get the piece of paper. If you succeed, you'll get a Map to the Time Capsule! Examine it, and you'll see that the Time Capsule is buried in the Playground.

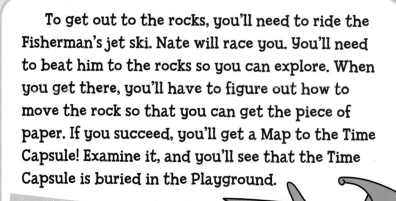

DIG, SPITSY, DIG

When you get to the Playground, you'll see that the girls are still talking, and they won't move no matter how hard you try. Don't they know that recess is over? If only you could ring the school bell . . . Oh, wait, you can! Go to the school and climb to the top. Use your bell clapper to ring the bell. The girls will leave the Playground.

You've still got one more problem. The Time Capsule is buried, and you don't have a Shovel. How can you dig it up? Then you remember how Spitsy the dog dug when you gave him Peanut Butter Crackers. Use your Crackers over the treasure spot, and Spitsy will dig up the Time Capsule.

There really is a treasure inside, and Nate will use it to save the school (although he really just wants to impress Gina). Go back to the school, and Mrs. Godfrey will give you the Island Medallion.

ASTR🪐KNIGHTS

DIFFICULTY: HARD

SYNOPSIS: THE TITLE TELLS YOU EXACTLY WHAT TO EXPECT ON THIS ISLAND: MEDIEVAL KNIGHTS IN OUTER SPACE! THERE'S A LOT GOING ON HERE. THE ISLAND IS BEING ATTACKED FROM THE SKY, A PRINCESS IS MISSING, AND A MYSTERIOUS INVENTOR HAS ESCAPED FROM PRISON. IF YOU CAN FIND THE PRINCESS AND SAVE THE ISLAND, YOU'LL MAKE THE KING AND QUEEN OF ARTURUS VERY HAPPY.

Did You Know?

Many Poptropicans think this is one of the most challenging Islands to complete. It's definitely a longer adventure than some other Islands, so you might want to save your progress often. The game automatically saves at certain points, but it doesn't hurt!

Poptropica

FIRST STOP: MAIN STREET

When you hop off the balloon, you'll see a sign that reads, "Welcome to Arturus." This place seems to be in trouble—there are burn marks on the ground and buildings. Some kind of battle has been going on here. Talk to the frightened villagers, and they'll tell you that invaders from the sky are attacking the village.

The first building you'll see is The House of Mordred or Mordred's Museum. You can go inside, and the curator will

THE CASTLE WAS ATTACKED BY INVADERS WHO CAME FROM THE SKY!

give you a Museum Pamphlet, but he won't let you explore unless you pay him one gold coin. You'll have to come back later. Read the pamphlet now, though. You'll learn that Mordred was put in prison because of his inventions, but he escaped.

Go outside and you'll pass a Fountain. The plaque on the Fountain is engraved with planets and stars on it. It reads, "In memory of Mordred, who brought technology to our land, but went astray."

Next is the Observatory. The Monk there will let you look through the Telescope, but that's about all you can do there. He tells you that the computers don't work because the kingdom has no power.

The last building on Main Street is the Crop Circle Inn, a multi-player room. Go past it to get to the Castle of Arturus.

THE REAL LEGEND OF MORDRED

MANY OF THE CHARACTERS ON THIS ISLAND ARE INSPIRED BY THE LEGEND OF KING ARTHUR—WHICH IS WHY THE KING AND QUEEN'S KINGDOM IS CALLED ARTURUS. MANY OF THE OLD STORIES ARE DIFFERENT, BUT MOST SCHOLARS AGREE THAT MORDRED WAS THE SON OF ARTHUR AND THAT HE BETRAYED HIS FATHER. WHEN ARTHUR LEFT ENGLAND TO FIGHT IN WALES, HE LEFT MORDRED IN CHARGE. MORDRED NAMED HIMSELF KING AND STOLE HIS FATHER'S THRONE.

THE HOUSE OF
MORDRED
- OR -
MORDRED'S
MUSEUM

EXPLORE THE CASTLE

Entering the castle is easy—you can walk right through the front doors. On the first floor, you'll find a door that leads to the Library. You can pick up two books there: *The Mystical Weapons of Arturus* and *The Life of Mordred—A Cautionary Tale*. Read both of these books to get clues to help you on your quest.

Head upstairs to the Throne Room and talk to the sad-looking King and Queen. The King will tell you that the invaders kidnapped the Princess. If you find her, he will make you a knight. The Queen will give you a clue: a scrap of paper with three different space coordinates on it.

X-73 Y-83

X-15 Y-15

X-83 Y-20

WHY ARE YOU SO UNHAPPY?

WHAT WAS THE PRINCESS UP TO?

WHERE DID YOU TAKE THE MESSAGES?

There's one more room to explore: the Lady-in-Waiting's Room. You'll see a Mechanical Mouse crawling around here. The Lady-in-Waiting looks very upset. Talk to her and she'll tell you that she helped the Princess send messages to a secret society. She left the messages on the Fountain on Main Street. She'll give you a secret message that the Princess wrote. But who was she sending the messages to?

I WAS ABLE TO SHOOT DOWN THREE OF THE INVADERS, BUT ONE ESCAPED!

Go outside the castle and the castle guards will let you shoot bolts from a giant crossbow. You'll notice that the bolts stick into a mysterious door on the castle wall. Hmm. Do you think there's a way in there?

FREE MANURE

Before you go back to the Fountain to learn more about the secret messages, go to the Muddy Field next to the castle. Talk to one of the peasants there, and he'll give you a free Bag of Manure.

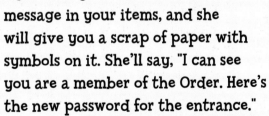

Keep walking and you'll come to Ye Olde Rumour Mille. The mill isn't working anymore, but you'll find a bunch of lazy villagers inside, gossiping. One of the girls will offer to exchange secret messages with you. Give her the secret

message in your items, and she will give you a scrap of paper with symbols on it. She'll say, "I can see you are a member of the Order. Here's the new password for the entrance."

Explore a little more before you leave the Muddy Field and you'll find a Coil of Rope. Be sure to add it to your Inventory.

THE SECRET ORDER HANGOUT

You're probably eager to learn more about the Secret Order, so go to the Fountain on Main Street. Click on the plaque with the outer-space symbols on it. The symbols on the paper that the girl in the mill gave you are the password to get into the order. Click on the symbols on the paper, then click on the big sun in the middle. A panel will open up, and you can enter the hangout.

Inside you'll find the disciples of Mordred. Talk to all of them. One of them will tell you that Mordred was hiding something in the top of the windmill. Another one will give you a Small Key that he says he found in Mordred's house.

Exit the hideout and splash around in the fountain water. You should find a Golden Coin. Now you can get into Mordred's Museum! But first, you should follow up on that clue the disciple gave you. What exactly is Mordred hiding in the top of the mill?

THE LANDSKIMMER

Go back to the mill and make your way to the top. Try hopping on the windmill blades to open up the glass door on the roof. In the Mill Attic, you'll find a landskimmer, a kind of hovercraft that can fly

TIP:
You'll need to climb the rope inside the mill before you can turn the windmill blades.

a few feet off the ground. It's out of fuel, but if you look in your items, you'll see the Bag of Manure. Use it, and the craft will fly out of the mill and land in the mud.

THE DARK DUNGEON

Go back to the Museum and give your coin to the curator. Click on the books, and he'll tell you that you can't take one—but he'll give you a Library Book Slip. The call number of the book is McM. Looks like it's time to go back to the castle Library!

Find the call number McM and click on the brick above it. This will open up the secret entrance to the Dungeon. In this creepy place you'll see a robot droid behind bars. You can try clicking on the handle on the wall, but it won't open the bars; it will open a door inside the cell wall. Before you leave, pick up the piece of Moldy Cheese on the floor.

When you leave the Dungeon, the Librarian will scold you for snooping, and the guards will block you from getting back in. Since you're in the castle, go back to the Lady-in-Waiting's Room and use the cheese to capture the Mechanical Mouse.

A CLUE FROM THE PRINCESS

There's still one room you haven't explored in the castle—the Princess's Room. That door on the outside castle wall must be a way in, but you can't jump to it. Look through your items and see if you have picked up something that can help you get in. That Coil of Rope might work, but you need some way to get it to attach to the wood door. Then you remember the crossbow and the bolts.

Click on the crossbow again, and you can attach the rope to one of the bolts. Shoot the bolt into the Princess's door and then climb across.

Look around until you find the Princess' Note. Read it and you'll learn that Mordred may have kept secrets under his bed. You can also read a page from the Princess's diary to learn more about her relationship with Mordred. Is it possible that she wasn't kidnapped? It looks like she might have fled with Mordred.

The order believes the Great Inventor kept many of his secrets under his bed, but the order dare not come out of their hiding place to seek them. I will do my best to aid them in their search, because I believe Mordred is alive! I've detected a beacon on a faraway planet, and I believe it may have come from him. I have sent a return signal, and

Head back to Mordred's Museum and go upstairs to see what's under the bed. You'll find a missing page from Mordred's Journal. He wrote, "I have found a nearby moon with much activity that I believe to be alien life! I have found that animal waste makes decent fuel, and there is just enough manure in Arturus to bring my flying craft to this moon." The page will also contain star coordinates for the moon.

Mordred has a spaceship? Maybe he's hidden it by the Muddy Field. There's a lot of manure there.

MORDRED'S UNDERGROUND LAB

When you go back to the mill, push the bales of hay around to see if anything's underneath. If you're successful, you'll reveal a hidden door. Use the Small Key to open it up.

Climb down and you'll find yourself in Mordred's Underground Lab. Click on the Mechanical Owl, and it will fly outside. What can you use to lure a robot owl? How about a Mechanical Mouse? Use it near the owl, and he will gulp it down and then start following you around.

Go back down into the lab and explore. Read Mordred's Journal and you'll learn that the owl's name is Merlin. You'll also learn more about why Mordred built his spaceship.

Push through the dirt wall on the left and you'll find yourself back in the Dungeon, but this time, you're in the cell with the robot droid. The droid will self-destruct when it sees you, and a Fuel Rod will fly out of its body and land on the other side of the bars. You can't fit through them—but Merlin can. Click on Merlin and then the rod, and he will retrieve it for you.

FYI. Click on the droid, and he will speak in binary numbers—a numerical system used by all computers.

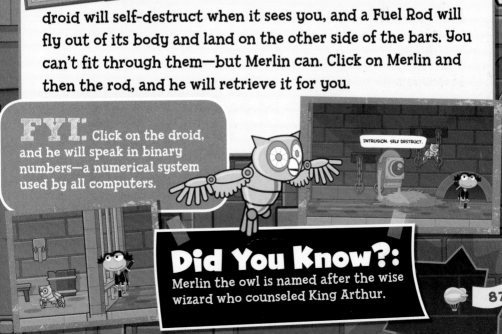

Did You Know?:
Merlin the owl is named after the wise wizard who counseled King Arthur.

So you didn't find the spaceship underground, but the Fuel Rod could be useful. Go back outside and hop inside the landskimmer. Head right and you will find a craft, a spaceship named Excalibur. Click on it and use the Fuel Rod to power it up. Since your goal is to find the Princess and stop the attacks on Arturus, you'll want to head to the moon you read about in Mordred's Journal. Enter the coordinates and then press the *Launch* button.

You're rocketing through space! The ship will most likely run out of fuel before you reach the Pewter Moon and you'll crash-land. When you exit the ship, you'll see that the moon is populated with little, green aliens. Talk to the one on the roof, and he'll tell you that he's looking out for an evil sorcerer called the Binary Bard. He's attacked the Pewter Moon and has created a fortress for himself on an unknown planet.

Go inside and talk to the Mechanic. He'll tell you how you can build your own rocket. You can build any kind of rocket you want here and fly it off the moon.

TIP:
A rocket with a good balance of speed and shields will be able to travel through space more effectively.

Did You Know?:
In the legend of King Arthur, Excalibur was a powerful, magical sword given to Arthur by the Lady of the Lake.

THE ICE PLANET

Remember those space coordinates the Queen gave you? You can enter one set of coordinates now. It doesn't matter where you go first. You may end up on the Ice Planet.

As you fly through space, you'll have to dodge asteroids and space sharks. Look at the scroll on the bottom of your control panel to see what's coming up next. It's tricky getting past the sharks, but you can get rid of them if you lure them into a black hole. Just be careful you don't get sucked in as well. The good thing is that once they're gone, they won't come back again.

Once you land on the Ice Planet, exit your spaceship and make your way across the icy platforms. Climb the mountain and you'll meet a knight named Sir Gawain. He'll tell you that he has been searching for the Princess. He believes a fierce creature is guarding her. He gives you a Force Shield so you can fight the beast.

The beast turns out to be a mechanical tiger that flies like a helicopter. It will shoot snowballs at you. After you defeat the Tiger Copter, Sir Gawain will join you on your quest. He'll tell you that two other knights are searching for the Princess: Sir Cador and Sir Pelleas.

TIP:

Use the Force Shield to bounce the snowballs back at the Tiger Copter. If your shields get damaged, you'll need to dodge the snowballs until they're back up.

TIP:

Getting through the obstacles in space can be hard on your spaceship's shields. They will recharge automatically after a short time as long as you avoid getting more damage. But if you need to get them up quickly, you can always transport back to the Pewter Moon to recharge them.

THE JUNGLE PLANET

Enter another set of coordinates, and you might end up on the Jungle Planet. Here you'll need to jump across some big flowers and swinging platforms to find Sir Cador. He'll tell you he thinks the Princess might be held in a cage hanging above a nest of eggs. He gives you a Laser Lance to help you rescue her.

When you jump across the eggs, robot baby phoenixes will hatch. Avoid them to get to the cage, where you'll find a Pegasus (a flying horse) inside. Open the cage with the laser and click on the Pegasus to ride it. As you try to escape, the Mother Phoenix will attack you. She'll shoot missiles at you, and you'll have to dodge them as well as flying bugs and storm clouds. Defeat her and Sir Cador will accompany you on your quest.

HINT:
Your laser works best when it is fully charged.

THE FIRE PLANET

Put in the last set of coordinates, and you may end up on the Fire Planet. (Once again, check your shields before you head there.) Exit your ship and you'll find that most of the planet's surface is made of bubbling hot lava. Jump from platform to platform until you reach the top of the volcano. Inside, you'll have to travel through the volcano's tunnels without getting hit by burning-hot steam. When you find a safe spot, wait patiently until the steam passes before moving on.

Get past the rock creature, and you'll meet the last knight, Sir Pelleas. He'll tell you that a beast has captured the Princess. Have you finally found her? To find out, you must slay the beast—a Mechanical Dragon—using the Ice Arrow he gives you. It won't be easy because the dragon will blast you with fireballs. If you succeed, Sir Pelleas will join your quest.

HINT:

There is a lever on the bottom of the dragon that opens the dragon's mouth. The Ice Arrow will do the most damage if you can get it inside the dragon's body.

MORDRED'S CITADEL

So you haven't found the Princess or Mordred or the mysterious Binary Bard yet. The knights will tell you about a gate located on a small asteroid. Navigate through a dangerous asteroid belt to reach the asteroid. If you get

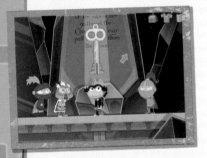

there safely, exit and climb on top of the mountain. You're now at the Crystal Gate. If you have all three knights with you, you can pull the Key from the stone and enter the Crystal Palace.

Inside, you'll see the Princess at last! She'll ask you for the knights' three weapons so she can destroy this evil place. But when you give them to her, she transforms into the Binary Bard. He'll laugh and tell you he will use the weapons to create the ultimate energy source so he can rule the universe. Then he'll escape through a stone wall.

You'll have to solve a puzzle to get through the wall. Inside, you'll see that the real Princess is trapped in a cylinder of green liquid on top of a tall platform. The Binary Bard reveals that he is actually Mordred. He's inside a huge Mecha robot fighting suit. You'll have to defeat him to save the Princess—and the universe.

Merlin will fly out to battle Mordred first, and you will control the owl during the battle. Then you will have to defeat Mordred on your own. If you succeed, the King will knight you and the Queen will give you an Island Medallion.

DEFEATING MORDRED

HAVING TROUBLE DEFEATING MORDRED IN THE FINAL BATTLE? HERE ARE SOME TIPS THAT MIGHT HELP:

1. WHEN YOU'RE BATTLING AS MERLIN, FLY DOWN AND PICK UP THE BLACK BOMBS. THEN FLY UP AND WAIT UNTIL THEY START TO TURN RED AND BLINK. THEN DROP THEM ON MORDRED.
2. IN THE SECOND PART OF THE BATTLE, YOU'LL NEED SOMETHING BIG TO TAKE DOWN MORDRED'S ROBOT SUIT. THE TWO LARGE CHANDELIERS HANGING FROM THE CEILING WILL DO THE TRICK. TO GET TO THEM, YOU'LL HAVE TO CLIMB UP TO THE PRINCESS.

THE BINARY BARD STARTED OUT AS A GOOD GUY, ORIGINALLY. HE WASN'T REALLY IMPORTANT TO THE STORY. THEN WE MADE HIS EYE RED, AND HE STARTED LOOKING MORE VILLAINOUS.—SHARK BOY, A POPTROPICA CREATOR

COUNTERFEIT ISLAND

DIFFICULTY: MEDIUM

SYNOPSIS: THE MUSEUM ON THIS ISLAND HOLDS SOME OF THE MOST FAMOUS WORKS OF ART IN THE WORLD. ONE OF THEM IS A PAINTING CALLED *THE SCREAM* BY EDVARD MUNCH. WORD ON THE STREET IS THAT A NOTORIOUS ART THIEF NAMED THE BLACK WIDOW IS PLANNING TO STEAL IT. CAN YOU STOP THE THEFT—OR WILL YOU BE CAUGHT UP IN A WHIRLWIND OF CRIME AND MYSTERY?

FIRST STOP: MAIN STREET

Everyone on the street is talking about *The Scream* and the rumor that someone is planning to steal it. Since you're right next to Museum Fantastique, head there to check out the painting. Outside, the Chief Inspector for the police will tell you she's on the lookout for the thief. You'll notice a Help Wanted sign on the museum door.

If you go in, the Security Guard will tell you it's not open yet. Before you leave, go outside and jump up to the museum roof, and you'll find a piece of a Torn Picture.

MUSEUM FANTASTIQUE

You might as well explore the Island while you wait for it to open. Head right and you'll meet a woman who greets you with, "Bonjour!" She tells you that the Black Widow is out to steal *The Scream*. Who is this Black Widow? And what's with the French greeting? While you ponder this, go inside the Web Browser Internet Café.

Inside, you can play an addictive game on the computer and pick up a Page from a French-English Dictionary. There's a Bearded Man who won't talk to you because he's absorbed in his game.

Next to the café is The Moldy Baguette Inn, a multi-player room. Outside you'll find a street artist who invites you to create your own masterpiece. You can print out your creation on your real-world printer. When you're done painting, explore the rooftops of Main Street and you'll find another piece of the Torn Picture.

STEALING *THE SCREAM*

NORWEGIAN ARTIST EDVARD MUNCH CREATED FIVE DIFFERENT VERSIONS OF *THE SCREAM*: TWO PAINTINGS; TWO PASTELS, WHICH ARE MADE WITH A CHALK-LIKE PIGMENT; AND ONE LITHOGRAPH, A PRINTED IMAGE. AT DIFFERENT TIMES, THE TWO PAINTINGS HAVE BOTH BEEN STOLEN! ONE WAS STOLEN FROM THE NATIONAL GALLERY OF NORWAY IN 1994. THE OTHER WAS STOLEN FROM THE MUNCH MUSEUM, ALSO IN NORWAY, IN 2004. BOTH STOLEN PAINTINGS WERE LATER RECOVERED.

CLOWNING AROUND DOWNTOWN

Head Downtown and the first stop you'll see is Bobo's Clown Store. There are two mimes outside—performers who act but don't speak. When you click on them, they'll move but they won't say anything. Inside the clown store you can get a free balloon. When you hold the balloon, you can jump higher (but more slowly), and it takes longer to get back to the ground.

Leave the clown store and walk to the Underground Tunnel tour. The Tour Guide will tell you that the Tunnel goes underneath the museum and out to the docks. Tickets are sold out. Next to the Tunnel entrance is a garbage can. If you look through the trash you'll find two tickets to the tour, but you can't use them yet.

Keep going and you'll find All that Jazz Café and the Police Station. There's not much going on here. This would be a good time to explore the Countryside.

> ☺**LOL:**
> If you jump to the roof of the clown store, you'll meet Bobo. He's hiding out because, as he says, "mimes really give me the creeps!"

MY TICKETS? THANK YOU! HERE, YOU CAN TAKE ONE FOR YOURSELF.

A SAD BOY AND A LOCKED HOUSE

In the Countryside you'll meet a crying boy and his mom. Click on her, and she'll speak to you in French. It's a good thing you have that Page from the French-English Dictionary! Use it and you'll figure out that the boy wants a balloon in a certain color. If you already have a balloon in that color, give it to the boy. If not, go

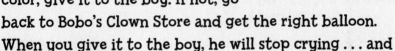

back to Bobo's Clown Store and get the right balloon. When you give it to the boy, he will stop crying . . . and then the balloon will lift him into the air! Maybe that wasn't such a good idea after all.

Run past the boy's shocked mother, and you'll come to the house of the Chief Inspector of the police. The door is locked. You've explored all you can here, so you might as well go back to the museum and see if it's open yet.

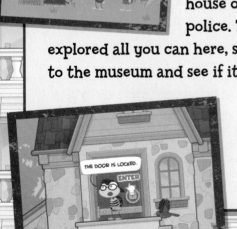

SECRET:

The sign on the Chief Inspector's house reads, "Inspector Veuve-Noire." You won't be able to translate this with your Dictionary Page. In French, *veuve-noire* means black widow.

THE UNDERGROUND TUNNELS

On your way to the museum you'll meet a guy who's very excited. "Did you hear about Balloon Boy? It's on the news inside." Go inside the Internet Café, and you'll see news footage of Balloon Boy on every television screen. The Bearded Man has stopped playing the game to watch the news. Talk to him, and he'll tell you he's lost his tickets to the Underground Tunnel tour. Give him the tickets you found in the trash, and he'll give you one ticket as a reward.

Go back to the tunnels and click on your items to use your ticket and get in. The Tour Guide will follow you into the dark tunnels. Click on her as you move and she'll tell you some useful stuff. Keep your eyes open and you'll find a piece of the Torn Picture. You may also spot what looks like the lid of a hatch with an image of a gargoyle head on it. You can try clicking on the hatch, but you can't get in.

When you exit the tunnels you'll be at the Docks. You'll see a Mysterious Man in a trench coat and hat.

He won't give you his name, but he'll tell you he's "somebody who knows too much." He tells you he knows who's going to steal *The Scream* and wants to stop the thief. He asks you to get a job at the museum and meet

him back at the Docks at nightfall. When you walk away from him, you'll encounter a bucket of fish and remark, "Something smells fishy." Can you really trust this guy?

Before you leave the Docks, look around and you'll find two more pieces of the Torn Picture.

THE LEGEND OF BALLOON BOY

ALTHOUGH HE NEVER SPEAKS A WORD, BALLOON BOY IS ONE OF THE MOST POPULAR CHARACTERS IN POPTROPICA. THAT'S BECAUSE MANY POPTROPICANS WERE LEFT WONDERING WHAT HAPPENED TO HIM. DID HE EVER LAND? NOBODY KNOWS, BUT IT'S POSSIBLE THAT BALLOON BOY MAY APPEAR ON ANOTHER ISLAND, SO KEEP WATCHING THE SKIES.

GET TO WORK

Go to the museum and ask the Security Guard about the help wanted sign. He'll tell you to talk to the Assistant Curator, who you'll find on the second floor. You'll also see *The Scream* on this floor.

The Assistant Curator will give you the job if you can help him put four paintings in the right spots in the museum. This test is easy to pass if you read the

signs that describe the paintings in each wing: the Cubism Wing, the Impressionism Wing, the Expressionism Wing, and the Realism Wing. Also, if you click on a painting, you'll get a clue about whether it's in the right spot.

Once you get the job, the Assistant Curator will bring you to the Forgery Detection Lab. Here, you'll learn how to discover if a painting is real or if it's been copied to look real. At the first station, you'll use an X-ray device and a microscope to examine some paintings. The third test requires you to use logic to examine a photograph. Take your time, and you should be able to pass these three tests.

HINT: The key to figuring out the photograph is to look at the moon and the stars.

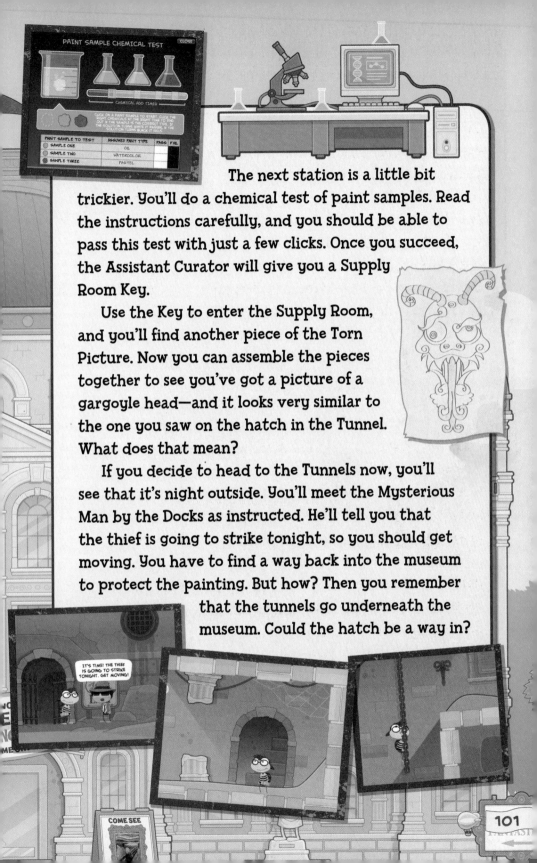

The next station is a little bit trickier. You'll do a chemical test of paint samples. Read the instructions carefully, and you should be able to pass this test with just a few clicks. Once you succeed, the Assistant Curator will give you a Supply Room Key.

Use the Key to enter the Supply Room, and you'll find another piece of the Torn Picture. Now you can assemble the pieces together to see you've got a picture of a gargoyle head—and it looks very similar to the one you saw on the hatch in the Tunnel. What does that mean?

If you decide to head to the Tunnels now, you'll see that it's night outside. You'll meet the Mysterious Man by the Docks as instructed. He'll tell you that the thief is going to strike tonight, so you should get moving. You have to find a way back into the museum to protect the painting. But how? Then you remember that the tunnels go underneath the museum. Could the hatch be a way in?

IT'S TIME! THE THIEF IS GOING TO STRIKE TONIGHT. GET MOVING!

COME SEE

THE GREAT BREAK-IN

Go back to the tunnels and make your way back to the hatch. Take the gargoyle picture out of your backpack. To get through the hatch, you'll have to rearrange the gargoyle's face to match the picture.

Go through the hatch, and you'll be in the museum's Supply Room. You're in! Use your Supply Room Key to get out of the room. Now you have to get to *The Scream* without the Security Guard spotting you. You'll have to avoid laser beams, too. Move quickly and look for places to hide.

When you reach *The Scream*, you'll hop on top of the light hanging over it so you can surprise the thief when they try to steal it. But things don't work out as you planned. Alarms go off and the Chief Inspector appears, flanked by two officers. They think *you're* the thief. You've been framed!

THE GREAT CHASE

You'll be taken to the police station where the Chief Inspector will question you the next morning. Pass the lie-detector test, and she will ask you to meet her in the museum's security office. When you get there, you'll be

able to look at the security footage for clues—except there are hours and hours of footage to view. If only you could narrow things down. Maybe something happened when the downstairs Security Guard left his post. You need to find him to ask him.

You'll find the Security Guard at Bobo's Clown Store. Talk to him and he'll give you his timecard. Use the numbers on the timecard to narrow down your search on the surveillance tape. When you do, you'll see the Mysterious Man in the footage!

Print out a picture of the screen, and the Chief Inspector will tell you to show the photo around town. Talk to the first mime, and she will act out someone playing music. That's a clue to check the Jazz café. You'll find the Mysterious Man inside, and he'll run away from you. The chase is on!

He'll jump on a scooter, and so will you. Chase him to the Docks, avoiding puddles, oil slicks, and other obstacles in the road. He will escape by boat, but he'll leave you a clue—a red Key Card with a black widow symbol on it.

Head back to the museum to tell the Chief Inspector what happened. When you do, the Assistant Curator will give you a package. It's a copy of *Starry Night* by Vincent Van Gogh and an X-ray device. Use the device to reveal a Secret Message under the painting. It's from the museum Curator. She tells you to meet her in the Pop Art Museum on Early Poptropica.

THE CURATOR'S SECRET

Head to your balloon and travel to Early Poptropica. Go to the Pop Art Museum. The Curator is an older woman wearing purple. She'll tell you that she has been hiding valuable paintings from the Black Widow for years. She's worried that Black Widow is getting close to finding them. She'll ask for your help and give you a Key. She'll also warn that someone you trust is watching you very closely.

Go back to Counterfeit Island and head for the only door still locked to you—the door of the Chief Inspector's house. You'll see a painting hanging high on the wall. Peel it away and you'll find the real painting of *The Scream* hiding underneath! Before you can do anything about it, you'll be knocked unconscious.

THE BLACK WIDOW REVEALED

You'll wake up tied to a chair in an underground hideout along with the Mysterious Man. The Black Widow will approach you, and she's someone you recognize. She thinks you know where the Curator is hiding the art. You'll tell her you don't know, and she'll leave the room angrily.

If you can escape your bonds, you can go after her. You'll have to get past her guards and use your Key Card to enter the Black Widow's Lair. To keep you at bay, the Black Widow will toss valuable works of art at you. You have to catch them. If more than one million dollars worth of art is destroyed, you'll fail this challenge. While you're trying to catch the art, you also have to try to crank the lever of a platform so you can reach the Black Widow and stop her.

If you succeed, the museum Curator will give you an Island Medallion. You'll get an extra bonus, too—she'll show you where the famous art is hidden.

TIP:

After the Black Widow throws four pieces of art, she'll rant and rave for a few seconds. That's just enough time to crank the platform handle before more art falls.

105

Reality 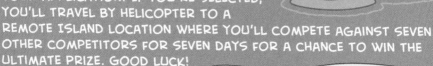 island

DIFFICULTY: MEDIUM

SYNOPSIS: HAVE YOU EVER WANTED TO BE A CONTESTANT ON A TELEVISION COMPETITION SHOW? NOW'S YOUR CHANCE! HEAD TO REALITY TV ISLAND TO PICK UP YOUR APPLICATION. IF YOU'RE SELECTED, YOU'LL TRAVEL BY HELICOPTER TO A REMOTE ISLAND LOCATION WHERE YOU'LL COMPETE AGAINST SEVEN OTHER COMPETITORS FOR SEVEN DAYS FOR A CHANCE TO WIN THE ULTIMATE PRIZE. GOOD LUCK!

FIRST STOP: MAIN STREET

Land in this TV-obsessed town, and you'll quickly learn that everyone is looking for a way to get on a reality TV show. Lots of people are talking about some guy named Bucky Lewis, a former reality-show contestant.

The first shop you'll find is TV World. Each television set is blaring a news report. Click on a screen to change the channel, and you'll see clips from the reality show. The address to mail in your Application appears on the screen: 123 Star Avenue, Hollywood. That's great— but you don't have an application.

FYI. The subject of the news report on TV is Counterfeit Island's own Balloon Boy!

106

To find an Application, you'll need to start exploring. The Island doesn't seem to be much bigger than Main Street. Go to Mike's Market, and you'll learn that Bucky was the first person voted off *Reality TV Island*. Inside is a man so excited about watching the show that he rushes out, dropping an issue of *Pop-Top!cs* magazine. Take it out of your items and read every page carefully. Inside, you'll find the Application you were looking for!

To fill out your Application and send it in, you'll need a Pen and a Stamp. You'll have to keep looking around for both of those.

BUCKY LEWIS, IN PERSON

Keep walking around and you'll find a Billiards Hall, a multi-player room. Next to that is The Wayside Motel. You can grab a Cheap Pen on the stand there. The owner will tell you that Bucky Lewis once stayed there. Maybe Bucky can help you with your Application. If you read the magazine carefully, you'll know what room he used to stay in. Go to that room and knock on the door.

You can knock, but no one will answer. Try all the doors, and the results will be the same. You have a feeling Bucky's got to be in there, though. There must be some way to get him to answer. Check the magazine again, and you'll see an ad for a pizza place. This could be just what you need.

Order a pizza and have it sent to Bucky's room. When the Pizza Delivery Guy arrives, you will offer to deliver the pizza yourself. Take it to Bucky's, and he will let you in his room.

Bucky looks like he's seen better days, and his room is a mess. He tells you it's a mistake to go on a reality show, but the lure of the grand prize is too strong for you. Bucky will give you the Postage Stamp you need.

Click on your application, and use the Cheap Pen to fill it out. Then use the Stamp and head for the nearest mailbox. The next day, you'll see a helicopter on top of the motel—and it's for you! You're going to be a contestant on the show! Hop into the helicopter and get ready to continue your adventure.

😄 LOL:
Try hopping on top of the helicopter blades and see what happens!

LEARN THE RULES

When you land on the remote island location, you'll learn the rules. The game starts out with eight contestants, including you. Each day, you'll compete in a challenge. After the challenge, each competitor will vote one person off of the island. If you win the challenge, you can't be voted off.

If you get voted off, you can go back to the helicopter and compete in the next season of the show. You can keep playing until you win and earn your Island Medallion.

MEET THE CONTESTANTS

Every season, you'll face seven contestants. The group will be different every time. Some of the contestants are familiar faces. Others are new. Here's a list of who you might be competing against:

Chef Jeff:
He's hungry for a win.

Betty Brownie:
She's going for the merit badge in kicking butt.

Dr. Hare:
He's the bunny-suit-wearing madman from 24 Carrot Island.

Betty Jetty:
She's the high-flying villain from Super Power Island.

Director D.:
He's the treacherous head of the B.A.D. organization.

Black Widow:
She's the international art thief from Counterfeit Island.

Freddy Fry:
His competitive juices are sizzling.

Brett Batter:
He's hoping for a grand slam.

Grandma Gracey:
She'll send a check for your birthday—a hip-check, that is.

Busy Bob:
He's all business when it comes to winning challenges.

Grandpa Grum:
His teeth may be false but his drive to win is totally real.

Cathy Codex:
She's got your number.

Helen Hiker:
There's no mountain
she can't climb.

 Richie Rebel:
You know he's a rebel because
he wears a motorcycle jacket.

 Hip Hop:
He thinks he can dance his
way to the top spot.

 Rickie Rock:
She pumps up the volume
in this competition.

 Hippie Harry:
Everything's groovy
until he betrays you!

 Sally Score:
Give her the ball and
she'll score a goal.

 Lassie Lasso:
She ties up her
opponents in knots.

 Sarah Snooty:
This rich girl thinks she
was born to win.

 Magic Mervin:
He's got a few tricks
up his sleeve.

 Sickly Skull:
Not even winning can make
this gloomy girl happy.

 Merry Muse:
To her, there's nothing
more poetic than victory.

 Slim Slam:
This basketball star has
some fast moves.

 Ned Noodlehead:
He's the comic book-store
owner from Super Power Island.

MASTER THE CHALLENGES

If you make it all the way to the end, you'll compete in seven challenges each season. Every time you return for a season, you'll get a new mix of challenges. The more you play them, the better you'll get at them. The best way to win the whole competition is to master the challenges so you cannot be voted out. Here's a list of challenges with a tip for winning each one:

★ Balanced Diet: Don't lose your cool when something new is added. You need to keep moving the cursor.

★ Boulder Push: Click as fast as you can to get these big rocks rolling.

★ Coconut Catch: Try to catch the coconuts that come in groups of three to bump up your total faster.

★ Geyser Guess: It takes luck to win this, not skill!

★ Hang Glider: Hang back from the other contestants a bit so you can see what's coming toward you. Let somebody else take the hit.

★ Knockout: See what plates the other players are targeting, and join up with them to eliminate the competition before you're eliminated.

- ★ On the Line: Plan ahead! Try to predict the movements of the fish when you see them.
- ★ Mountain Race: Stay as close to the front of the screen as possible.
- ★ Pole Climb: Don't be fooled by all the poles. The best way to win is to jump between two of them the whole time.
- ★ Shot Put: The best angle for each shot is a little bit above the center line. Also, make sure you're at full power when you click on the power bar.
- ★ Shuffleboard: It's good to get your puck close to the target—but knocking your opponents' pucks away from the target is just as important.
- ★ Totem Hop: Your totem will shake before it drops. Don't jump the gun!
- ★ Turtle Shell Toss: Once you make a successful throw, don't move your cursor again.
- ★ Water Run: The pig will knock you over and spill your jug every time, so steer clear.

GET A VOTING STRATEGY

After each challenge, the contestants will each vote for the one contestant they want voted off the island. When it's voting time, you can click on the contestant you want to vote off. The votes will be announced one by one, and you'll get to see who votes for you. If you're lucky, somebody else will be voted off, and you'll get to stay.

If you make it through the first round, pay attention to the voting tally. Many contestants vote for the same person each round. If one of the contestants gets a few votes, vote for them next time. That way, your vote will join the others', and the other contestant may get voted off instead of you.

Also, be careful who you vote for. They may just vote for you during the next round!

TAKE HOME THE PRIZE

When you get to the last challenge, you have to beat your opponent to win the prize. There's no final vote. If you succeed, you'll win your Island Medallion. If not, you can come back for another season and try again!

MYTHOLOGY island

DIFFICULTY: HARD

SYNOPSIS: TRAVEL BACK IN TIME TO A LAND WHERE GODS RULED THE WORLD AND MONSTERS LURKED BEHIND EVERY CORNER. THE MIGHTY ZEUS IS LOOKING FOR A HERO TO COMPLETE A QUEST FOR HIM. IF YOU CHOOSE TO ACCEPT IT, YOU'LL FACE MANY DANGERS IN ORDER TO SUCCEED. BUT BE CAREFUL—IMMORTALS ARE TRICKY AND CAN'T ALWAYS BE TRUSTED.

FIRST STOP: MAIN STREET

When you jump off the blimp, you'll find yourself in a land that looks like Ancient Greece. There's a sign to your left pointing to the Tree of Immortality. It looks tempting, but before you check it out, go right next door to the Museum of Olympus. There, you'll learn about the history of Zeus, Poseidon, and Hades. You can also learn about the different gods and goddesses by reading their statues. Make sure you go to the second floor, where you can get the Starfish.

Now you're ready to see what's up with the Tree of Immortality. At the base, you'll find an old woman who gives you a mysterious message. There are signs all over warning you not to pick an apple, but you ignore them. You're too curious. Climb to the top until you find the god Pan. Take his challenge, and if you succeed, he'll show you a path to the Golden Apple.

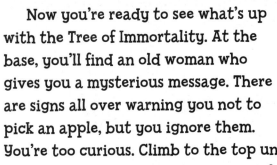

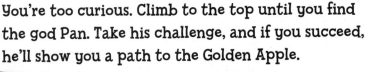

TIP:

The mushrooms on the tree are bouncy, and the snakes are friendly.

MAKE A DEAL WITH ZEUS

When you pick up the apple, Zeus, the king of the gods, will descend from Mount Olympus. He's pretty angry with you, but it's your lucky day. Instead of turning you into a newt, he's willing to make a deal with you. If you bring him five rare items, he will forgive you—and make you immortal, to boot. It's an offer you can't refuse. Zeus gives you the Sacred Items Scroll.

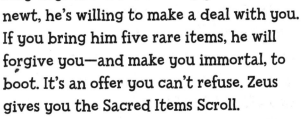

The scroll tells you which five items you need to find:

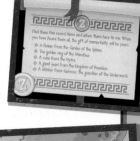

★ A Flower from the Garden of the Sphinx
★ The Golden Ring of the Minotaur
★ A Scale from the Hydra
★ A Giant Pearl from the Kingdom of Poseidon
★ A Whisker from Cerberus, the Guardian of the Underworld

Head back down the tree to start your search. The old woman will transform into the goddess Athena, who is Zeus's daughter. She'll warn you that you can't trust her father. She'll suggest that her brother Hercules might be able to help you, if you can convince him. She also says that she will help you on your quest—just look to the olive trees.

You noticed that the Garden of the Sphinx is to your left. But before you go there, you decide to see if you can get Hercules to help you. Head back to Main Street.

AN UNWILLING HERO

It's easy to find Hercules—he's inside Herc's Hero Hut, selling autographs. He's pompous, and he's more interested in selling you a picture than helping you. Looks like you're on your own.

Talk to people on Main Street, and you'll hear some good gossip about Zeus and his brothers. You'll also meet a guy who really loves his goat. But there's no time to chat. Head to the Garden of the Sphinx and see if you can get one of the Sacred Items.

SORRY, KID. I NEED A BETTER REASON THAN THAT TO LEAVE THIS COMFY SPOT.

THE PUZZLE OF THE SPHINX

In the Garden of the Sphinx you'll find the sleeping Sphinx, half-woman, half-beast. Click on her, and she will give you a challenge—get the water flowing in her aqueduct, and she'll give you a flower. You'll need to jump up on the levers to move the pieces of the aqueduct. Connect them, and water will flow down and water the dried-up flower below the Sphinx, reviving it. The Sphinx will keep her promise and give you the Rare Flower. You'll notice a scrap of paper with some words on it, but they don't make sense. Are they part of some kind of secret message?

Before you leave the garden, pick a Pomegranate from the tree above the Sphinx. You'll also find the door to the Minotaur's Labyrinth here, but you can't get in. You may notice an olive glowing on a tree next to the door. Click on it, and Athena will appear and give you advice: "Music can open up new doors."

FREE! YOU PICK EM YOU KEEP EM

MUSIC CAN OPEN UP NEW DOORS.

THE MAZE OF THE MINOTAUR

Go back to Main Street and head for the Grove of Temples. On the way there you'll pass the Atlas Gym, a multi-player room. You'll also see the gates of Mount Olympus, but you can't enter unless you're accompanied by an immortal.

Get to the Grove of Temples, and the first temple you'll come across is the Temple of Apollo. Inside, there are statues of the nine muses who inspire the arts. Get a free Reed Pipe, then click on the muse holding a Reed Pipe—Euterpe. Talk to her, and she will teach you a Pipe Tune.

Go back to the Garden of the Sphinx and approach the door to the Minotaur's Labyrinth. Use your Reed Pipe to open the door. You'll meet the Minotaur, half-human, half-bull. The Ring you need is in his nose, but he won't do you any favors until you enter his Labyrinth. Luckily, Athena gives you a golden thread so you won't lose your way.

Inside the Labyrinth, you'll have to make your way through the maze, solve a ghostly puzzle, avoid stinging scorpions, and deal with hissing snakes. If you succeed, you'll get the Ring from the Minotaur. There's another scrap of paper with words on it.

You have two items, but you need to find three more. You know that two of them can be found with Poseidon and Hades. Going back to the Grove of Temples is a good idea.

TIP:
In the snake challenge, keep a look out for the snake with the red eyes. Click on it three times to win.

DESCENT INTO THE UNDERWORLD

When you get to the Temple of Hades, you'll see it's covered with graffiti. Help the man clean off the graffiti and he'll give you one Drachma—a gold coin.

The entrance to the Underworld is inside the temple. To get in, you'll need to leave an offering. Look in your items. Those Pomegranates are just the thing. Jump down, and you'll land in the River Styx with Charon, who brings the dead to the Underworld. Your

journey will be dangerous, but if your reflexes are fast, you'll make it to the other side.

When you land, you'll find a three-headed dog named Cerberus guarding the entrance. Getting a Whisker from him is impossible while he's awake. What could put him to sleep? Try playing the Pipe Tune. If Cerberus falls asleep, you can get the Whisker from him. You will see the entrance to Hades's Throne Room, but it's blocked by a heavy stone.

Now you can leave the Underworld. Head back to the Grove of Temples and enter the Temple of Poseidon.

TIP:
Jump over any alligators you see. You can jump or duck to avoid the flaming skulls.

TIP:
Ride the geyser to get to Poseidon's Temple.

AN ITEM IN THE DEEP

Check your items for an offering that will get you into this watery kingdom. How about a Starfish? Poseidon's kingdom is a sandy beach by the ocean. The lifeguard, Triton, is Poseidon's son. Talk to people on the beach and you'll meet Aphrodite, the goddess of beauty. Pass her test and she'll give you the Touchscreen Mirror. This mirror can transport you to the major realms of the gods.

You know you're looking for a pearl from a giant clam, so jump into the water. Make your way through the maze of coral until you find the clam. Grab the giant pearl. Swim a little farther and you'll see a sign that reads, "Gnarly Monster Inside!" Could this be the cave of the Hydra?

Swim inside and you'll find the five-headed monster. You'll have to stomp on each of the heads in order to get the Hydra's scale. When you're done, you can use the Touchscreen Mirror to exit the

TIP:
Go back to the Museum of Olympus and read the statues to pass Aphrodite's test.

cave. You need to find Zeus to give him the five items, so head back to the Tree of Immortality. If you decide to swim around before you go, you'll see the entrance to Poseidon's Throne Room. Another big rock is blocking the way in.

TRICKED!

Athena will meet you at the base of the tree. She shows you that the words attached to each of the Sacred Items can be pieced together to form a clue: "Whoever wields the five Sacred Items will rule all of Poptropica." That doesn't sound good. Zeus appears and scoffs at you, a foolish mortal. He was just using you to get the five Sacred Items. He's not giving you immortality, either. He steals the items and goes back to Mount Olympus.

Athena tells you that you must defeat Zeus, and you need the powers of Poseidon and Hades to do it. But how will you get into their Throne Rooms? You've got to convince Hercules to help you. Go back to Herc's Hero Hut and talk to him. He's glad you have the Touchscreen Mirror so he doesn't have to do a lot of walking, and he agrees to come with you.

GATHER YOUR WEAPONS

Hercules is strong enough to move the rocks blocking the two Throne Rooms. Talk to Poseidon and get Poseidon's Trident. Talk to Hades and get Hades's Crown. Then head to Mount Olympus. It's time to fight Zeus!

Since you're with Hercules, you can get through the gates. On the way up, Hercules will encounter a little problem, and you'll be on your own. Use the Drachma you earned cleaning Hades's temple to buy a Bag of Wind from Aeolus. This will get you to the top of the mountain.

TAKE THAT, ZEUS!

The only way to get the items back is to battle Zeus. If you wear Hades's Crown and hold Poseidon's Trident, you will grow to the size of a god and be able to fly. Zip around on pink clouds and try to zap Zeus with the trident. If Zeus hits you, you will lose a pink cloud. Lose all of your clouds, and you'll have to start the battle over—so grab a pink cloud whenever you see one!

If you succeed, Zeus will give up the items, and Athena will give you your Island Medallion.

SECRET:

After you defeat Zeus, put on Hades's Crown. If you hit the space bar while wearing the crown, you will become god-sized. Have fun towering over other Poptropicans!

123

SKULLDUGGERY ISLAND

DIFFICULTY: HARD

SYNOPSIS: AHOY THERE, MATEYS! IF YOU'VE ALWAYS WANTED TO SAIL THE SEAS IN SEARCH OF PIRATE TREASURE, THEN CLIMB ABOARD THIS ISLAND. YOU'LL GET A TREASURE MAP, SAIL YOUR OWN SHIP, ASSEMBLE A CREW, AND TRADE TO EARN COINS. WHEN YOUR SHIP IS READY, YOU'LL ENGAGE IN A FIERCE BATTLE WITH A NOTORIOUS PIRATE. SO STRAP ON YOUR EYE PATCH AND GET READY FOR THE ADVENTURE OF A LIFETIME!

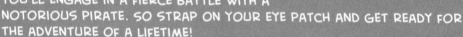

FIRST STOP: MAIN STREET

Hop onto the dock at Fort Ridley, and you'll meet a kid who tells you, "When I grow up, I want to sink Captain Crawfish." As you look around, you'll see that the fort is badly damaged. A soldier tells you the fort was attacked. Was this Captain Crawfish responsible?

Climb up to the tower, and the old sailor there will tell you he needs a way to signal ships. If you look through the Telescope right now you may see a ship on the horizon. Could this be Captain Crawfish?

THERE'S A PIRATE PATROLLING THE WATERS!

This is a good time to explore Main Street. You'll meet a villager who has no money to buy feed for his chickens. Talk to the woman on the street and she'll tell you that Captain Crawfish is indeed the one responsible for attacking the town. He and his crew have stolen everything valuable!

You'll pass the Broken Barrel, a multi-player room. Then you'll see the General Store. The man on the porch will tell you about a Treasure Map that people are looking for. Inside, you'll find some Grain, which is perfect for feeding chickens. But you don't have any money to buy it. You can, however, pick up a Broken Mirror for free. When you're done with the General Store, head for the Bridge.

VISIT THE GOVERNOR

When you cross the Bridge, you'll meet a woman who says she threw a coin in the water and made a wish. Climb down to the water and swim under the bridge until you find the coin. You can use this to buy Grain in the General Store.

Because you're a nice person, you will give the Grain to the villager so he can feed his chickens. He'll give you a chicken to thank you. Now head back across the Bridge. You'll meet a farmer who tells you that the pests are eating his crops, and he has no way to feed his family. Check your items to see if you have anything that can get rid of bugs. A hungry chicken should do the trick. Give it to him, and he'll give you a Blue Candle in return.

Keep going right. A villager will tell you that Governor Roland has found an interesting document. That's a good reason to go to the Governor's Mansion. Outside you'll see the grave of Governor Ridley.

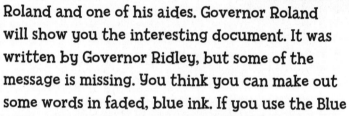

Inside you'll find Governor Roland and one of his aides. Governor Roland will show you the interesting document. It was written by Governor Ridley, but some of the message is missing. You think you can make out some words in faded, blue ink. If you use the Blue Candle now, you can read the entire message.

You'll learn that before he died of old age, Governor Ridley hid the town's treasure. He made a Map that shows where the treasure is buried and hid it on five nearby islands. He warns that it's only safe to bring the pieces of the Map back to Fort Ridley after Captain Crawfish is defeated.

Governor Roland says that if you find the Map pieces and vanquish Captain Crawfish, he'll give you the Key you need to find the treasure. It sounds like a good deal. Too bad you don't have a ship.

Leave the Governor's Mansion and climb down to the shore to see if you can find a ship. You'll meet a woman

who says her husband, a merchant, has been lost at sea for months. She wishes there was some way to signal his ship safely to the docks.

That gives you an idea. You quickly head back to the signal tower on top of the fort.

HEY! THERE'S A RAFT OUT THERE!

BEGIN YOUR JOURNEY

I HAVE FOUND MY WAY TO MY WIFE AND HOME, THANKS TO YOU!

Look in your items for something you could use to signal a ship. How about that Broken Mirror? It may be broken, but it can still reflect light. Look into the Telescope until you see a floating raft. Use the mirror to signal it. Then head to the Docks.

You'll be greeted by the grateful merchant, who has been lost at sea. He'll thank you by giving you his raft. When you board, you'll find two crew members waiting for you: the kid who wants to get even with Captain Crawfish and the old sailor from the signal tower.

Take some time to read the helpful tips he gives you:

★ Visit the trading posts on the different Islands, and trade wisely.
★ Head to the shipyards on Dragon Cove to upgrade your ship.
★ Keep an eye out for new crew members.
★ If you need a loan, go to the Golden Harbor Bank.

FINALLY, I CAN RETURN TO THE HIGH SEAS!

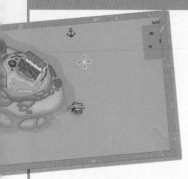

You might be eager to battle Captain Crawfish right away, but you can't do that in a crummy raft. You'll need a big, well-equipped ship and a talented crew. To get those, you'll need doubloons. And to get doubloons, you'll need to trade.

You can trade for silk, spices, grain, or medicine. You already have some cargo on your ship that you can trade. The key to trading is to sell your goods for as much money as you can get, and buy new goods as cheaply as you can. That way, you can make a profit.

To see how much money and goods you have, click on the ship icon on the bottom left of your screen.

TIP:
Your ship can only hold so much cargo. You may have to sell some goods before you buy new ones.

SET SAIL

Hit your spacebar to drop anchor and set sail. Use the mouse to move your ship. Avoid storms and other obstacles in the water. Pick up floating cargo if you see it and you'll earn extra goods and doubloons.

It doesn't matter which Island you visit first, but it's a good idea to go to Dragon Cove first and check out the ship builders there. Then you can find out how many doubloons you'll need to raise. Each time you upgrade your ship, you'll move faster through the water and withstand damage more easily. You can also hold more cargo, which is important if you want to keep trading.

These are the upgrades you can get:

JIMMY RIGGER:
3,000 DOUBLOONS

CARABELLE:
9,000 DOUBLOONS

SEA SULTAN:
30,000 DOUBLOONS

KOI:
90,000 DOUBLOONS

SEA FURY:
300,000 DOUBLOONS

PHOENIX WARBIRD:
1,000,000 DOUBLOONS

You're going to have to do a lot of trading to raise that much gold! You'd better get busy. And don't forget—you need to look for the missing Map pieces, too.

DRAGON COVE

You'll need to head down to the water here to find the missing Map piece. Stand on the head of the statue and you will get the Mallet. You'll quickly figure out that you can use the Mallet to ring the nearby bell. When you ring the bell, fish jump out of the water. Help the Fisherman catch the fish by pushing him to the right spot and he'll give you a piece of the Skullduggery Archipelago Map.

On this Island you'll find an Expert Shipbuilder willing to join your crew, but you can't hire him until you get enough coins.

TIP:
The Trader at Dragon Cove buys spices for a high price and sells silk cheaply.

BOUFFANT BAY

When you land here, a pirate will tell you that he heard a piece of the Map was hidden at 312 Hanging Fern Way, but there's no such address. Head down the street to see if you can find the house. You may notice three fern plants hanging from a building's balcony. Try clicking on them to see what you find.

HINT:
The key to clicking on the ferns is in the address: 3-1-2. If you succeed, you'll get the piece of the Map you were looking for. Then go inside Willard's Warehouse and you'll meet someone who is willing to become your Cargo Master. You'll need to get more coins before you can hire him.

TIP:
The Trader at Bouffant Bay buys silk for a high price and sells medicine cheaply.

PARROT PORT

A chatty parrot in this port will give you clues that will lead you to the missing Map piece. Near the end of your search, you'll need to find a tasty treat to lure him to you. Look around Petey's Pirate Pub and see if you can find a Cracker.

You can find a Navigator for your ship here, but you need to have enough coins to hire her.

TIP:
The Trader at Parrot Port buys medicine for a high price and sells spices at a decent price.

GOLDEN HARBOR

The sky glows orange in this exotic harbor. You'll have to help the villagers fix a problem with their lights in order to get the missing Map piece. Each time you turn one light on, two others turn off. Keep playing with the pattern until

it matches the pattern above the archway on one of the buildings. After you get the lights working, head over to the Golden Harbor Bank.

Inside the bank, you can take out a loan to help you upgrade your ship more quickly. You'll have to pay the money back in twenty days, with interest, but it's worth it because you can earn more money with a larger ship.

TIP:
The Trader at Golden Harbor pays a decent price for spices and silk and sells grain very cheaply.

This dark and spooky outpost looks dangerous. Ask around and you'll learn that the missing Map piece is in a "cavity in the cove." You know that a cavity can be a hole in the earth or a mountain. It can also be in a tooth. When you think you've found the hiding place, you'll need to find a way to blast it open.

Head to Corsair Cannonry. You can hire a Cannoneer for your ship here. You can also get a Cannon Starter Kit. All you need are some explosives, and you can get the final piece of the Map.

TIP:

The Trader at the Pirate Outpost buys grain for a good price and sells spices fairly cheaply.

HINT:

The easiest way to earn coins quickly is to start at Dragon Cove and sail from island to island in a clockwise circle. That way you'll maximize how many coins you earn from each trade.

BATTLE CAPTAIN CRAWFISH

When you have all of your crew and have bought the Phoenix Warbird, you are ready to battle the dreaded Captain Crawfish. Look at the Map and you will see a hidden Island: Skullduggery Island. Sail down there and you will encounter Captain Crawfish's ship. Get ready for a blazing cannon battle on the waves.

Once you sink his ship, it's safe to return to Fort Ridley and see Governor Roland. He will give you a Bone Shovel and show you exactly where to find the treasure on Skullduggery Island.

Travel back to the Island and follow the instructions until you come to the right spot. Then use your Shovel to dig. You'll uncover your treasure—and, to your surprise, Captain Crawfish! The Governor's aide was actually a spy all along.

Luckily, your faithful crew is nearby, and they take down Captain Crawfish for good. Return the treasure to Fort Ridley, and Governor Roland will give you an Island Medallion.

SKULLDUGGERY MEDALLION

AND NOW, IT IS TIME TO CLAIM MY TREASURE!

Save

STEAMW⚙RKS ISLAND

DIFFICULTY: MEDIUM

SYNOPSIS: WHEN YOU LAND, YOU'LL QUICKLY SEE THAT THIS ISLAND IS NOT LIKE ANY OTHER YOU'VE EVER VISITED. THE PLACE IS DESERTED AND OVERGROWN WITH GIGANTIC VINES. THERE ARE OLD ROBOTS AND MACHINE PARTS EVERYWHERE, AND THE BUILDINGS ARE ALL MADE UP OF GEARS, LEVERS, AND ENGINES. WHAT IS THIS PLACE, AND WHERE ARE ALL THE POPTROPICANS? SOLVING THIS MYSTERY MAY BE YOUR GREATEST CHALLENGE YET.

FIRST STOP: MAIN STREET

The first thing you'll notice is that there is nobody to talk to when you land. You'll see a broken robot in front of the Clockwork Cantina. Click on it and see if you can fix it. If you succeed, you'll get a Multi-Tool. Climb to the roof of the cantina and pull a switch, and that will cause a steel beam to extend so you can climb higher.

Jump from the beam onto the clouds of steam, and they will shoot you up to the top of the next building. You'll see a pipe with a glass dome covering it.

Use your Multi-Tool to open it up and you'll drop down into the Mayor's Office. Click around and you'll learn a little bit more about what might have happened here. Mayor Crumb's Note implies that the whole Island was in danger. At the end, you'll find a number that you'll need to remember later.

By now, you're starting to realize that you're going to have to try out everything you see as you explore this place. Climb back down to the street. Dig through the Garbage Bin and you'll find a Steam Battery. Next door you'll find the Steamworks Center and Museum. To explore the second floor, you'll need to raise the arm of the yellow machine on the right. Look around and you'll find a Dirty Beaker.

Exit the museum and you'll find a multi-player room next door: The Steamworks Gear Shop. Now that you're done with Main Street, head left to Gear Alley.

A STEAMWORKS STRATEGY

ON THE OTHER ISLANDS, YOU GET CLUES ABOUT WHAT TO DO NEXT BY TALKING TO THE ISLAND'S INHABITANTS. ON STEAMWORKS, YOU'LL HAVE TO GET YOUR CLUES FROM THE MACHINES. BE SURE TO CLICK ON EVERY MACHINE, GEAR, OR LEVER YOU COME ACROSS.

ALSO, CHECK YOUR ITEMS FREQUENTLY. IF YOU'RE STUCK, THERE MAY BE AN ITEM YOU CAN USE TO ESCAPE YOUR SITUATION.

GEAR ALLEY

The first building you'll see here is Sully's Steam-Powered Paraphernalia. The door is locked, so walk to the blue building next door, the Living Quarters. You won't be able to get in here, either, but you can explore outside. Make sure to get the Robot Crab and Sully's Key from the roof.

The rooftops on Gear Alley hold another prize: an Old Vine. Make sure to pick it up when you find it.

HINT:
The crab will really *flip* if you jump on him.

BACK TO SULLY'S SHOP

Now that you have Sully's Key, go back to Sully's Steam-Powered Paraphernalia. There is a Steam Terminal next to the entrance. The shape of the terminal is the same as your Steam Battery. Use the battery in your items to open the door. You'll have to solve a puzzle to power up the battery first.

TIP:
The battery puzzle looks complicated, but it's really just simple math. Just keep adding and subtracting numbers until you get to your goal number.

Once you're inside, you'll find a robot sleeping in the corner. Look for something you can use to wake him up. The frightened robot won't talk to you at first, but he will follow you around. Before you leave the room, pick up a rubber Mallet.

Outside, you'll see that the entrance to Sully's Garage is open. Inside, you'll find a cool-looking robot called a Mech. It seems to be missing some parts: a Steam Motor and a Mech Crank.

THE HUB

The only place left to explore is that deserted area with the bridge—the Hub. There you'll find a red-hot metal hatch. If only you had something to cool it down with! Look in your Items, and you'll see that the Robot Crab's tank is filled with cool water. It's just what you need.

Head down the hatch, and the robot will follow you. There is a highway of large pipes in this dark, underground area—and something is moving inside them. A scary-looking plant monster will block your path. Time to check your items again! Try using the Old Vine in combination with some hot steam.

Once you kill the plant, you'll be able to get to an elevator. Solve a puzzle and you'll hear something being powered up.

"STEAMWORKS WAS MY FAVORITE ISLAND TO WORK ON BECAUSE IT'S SUCH A UNIQUE ENVIRONMENT. I STUDIED MACHINES WITH INTERESTING CONFIGURATIONS OF PIPES AND GEARS TO GET IDEAS."—VLAD THE VIKING, A POPTROPICA CREATOR

THE CAPTAIN'S CABIN

Now it's time to exit the underground area and explore the Hub some more. You can try jumping to the very top, but you won't be able to get all the way. Look around for a solution. There's a large wheel on the front of the Hub that could get you where you need to go, but it's not moving. If you can get it moving, you can get to the top of the Hub. There, you'll find the entrance to the Captain's Cabin.

Plant vines will immediately ensnare the robot who's been following you. Find a way to free him, and he'll speak to you for the first time. He'll tell you his name is Sprocket, and he's a Sidekick-Bot. His best friend, Zack, disappeared along with everyone else on the Island. Before he vanished, Zack was reconstructing an old Mech.

SPROCKET! SIDEKICK-BOT, MODEL 9883. FRIEND TO ZACK.

Sprocket will show you a hologram of what Zack looks like. You realize that Zack must have created that cool robot you saw in Sully's Garage.

On the wall you'll see a copy of the painting that you saw in the Mayor's Office. That reminds you—you learned a code there. Could it be useful here?

Yes, it could be. Click on the dial on the bottom of the painting and enter the code. A secret door

CENTER AND MUSEUM

will open, and you can enter Captain Ziggs's Room. Here you'll find the Bridge Key and the Weed Whacker. You'll find a Note from Ziggs that reads, "I raised the drawbridge to keep those things at bay." What things? You're starting to get an idea that the Island was attacked by creatures of some kind. Were they robots? Or were they related to that plant monster you found in the pipes?

Ziggs's Note reminds you of the bridge you saw earlier. Head there now.

THE PRODUCTION ZONE

To lower the bridge, you'll need to power up the Steam Terminal, using the Steam Battery as you did before. Cross the bridge, and you'll see a machine with a large wrecking ball on the end. Figure out how to drop a wrecking ball, and you'll create a hole. Looks like it leads somewhere . . .

THE FACTORY AND THE GREENHOUSE

Drop down into the hole, and you'll enter a factory room that houses a large machine. Activate the machine by jumping on the large buttons. Once the machine gets moving, you can use it to get to the top of the room. Look around to find the Mech Steam Motor. This must be a part for the Mech that Sprocket told you about.

Keep going up, and you'll end up in the Greenhouse. Here you can make Herbicide—stuff that kills plants. You can see how that would be useful in a place like this. It's a good thing you found that Beaker earlier. Use the chart on the wall to help you figure how much of each chemical to add to the Beaker.

You've made the Herbicide just in time—if you go farther, you'll encounter a plant monster with snapping jaws. Use the Herbicide on it and see what happens.

😄 LOL:
Check out the chalkboard in the Greenhouse to see a reference to one of the characters from Super Power Island.

Get past this monster and you'll find an old Janitor Robot. Get the Living Quarters Access Key from him. When you do, he'll wake up and alarms will start blaring. You need to find a way out that's not blocked by security measures. Try clicking on any doors that you see. If your way out is blocked, see what's in your items that can help you break through. How about that rubber Mallet?

saving game

This is a good time to get in the Living Quarters building. Go back to Gear Alley. Once again, you'll need to power up your Steam Battery to get inside. Work your way up and look for Zack's Room.

Look around to find more information about the Mech that Zack built. There's a puzzle on the wall. Solve it and you can go outside and get the Mech Crank. Now you have the missing parts you need to fix the Mech!

Go to Sully's Garage and use the Mech Steam Motor and the Mech Crank to fix the robot. Jump inside and you'll see that you can control the Mech's movements.

You're a giant robot! Cool! You'll also get a Teleporter so you can instantly return to the Mech any time you leave it.

To exit the garage, you'll need to cut through some thick vines. Good thing you have that Weed Whacker. Use it and it will attach to the Mech.

THESE ENORMOUS WEEDS ARE BLOCKING THE ENTRANCE.

FIND THE LOST INHABITANTS

Now you need to find out what happened to Zack, the Mayor, and all the other inhabitants of the Island. Use the Mech to explore these new rooms. Hit your spacebar to attack them with your Weed Whacker. This device can also deflect any blasts the plants shoot at you.

Keep going and you'll find the blades of a giant windmill blocking a door. You'll have to leave the Mech to jump to the top of the structure and use your Multi-Tool to stop the blades from moving. Then you can hop back in the Mech, and you and Sprocket can go through the door.

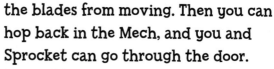

THE DOOR IS BLOCKED BY THIS LARGE SAIL.

You'll enter a dark, creepy place— the Hibernation Chamber. Find a way to light up the room, and you'll find Zack and the others! Mayor Crumb will explain things to you. The people of the Island performed plant experiments that went horribly wrong. They went into hibernation to protect themselves. That was two hundred years ago!

You'll hear some menacing noises beneath you. The plant monsters that once terrorized the Island are still alive and well. You've got to find their center—the plant brain—to stop them once and for all.

This might be the most dangerous mission you'll ever face. Before you embark, make sure to get the Toxic Blaster and attach it to your Mech. You'll need it.

MECH VS. THE PLANT MONSTERS!

You'll have to make your way through monster-filled tunnels to get to the main plant monsters. A moving platform will take you there. The room contains three monsters, each on a different level. There is acid on the floor, so be careful—if you fall into it, you have to start over.

The first monster will lash out at you with its legs. The second monster will use its legs and shoot seed pods at you. When you battle the third monster, you'll have to deal with plant bombs dropping on you from above as well.

Defeat all three of them and the Mayor will give you an Island Medallion.

TIP:

Simply using your Toxic Blaster on the monsters won't defeat them. When you're fighting a monster, bump into it. It will extend its neck to attack you. When that happens, duck to avoid the head by holding your mouse button and clicking underneath your character. Then press the spacebar to shoot.

OUCH!!!

OUCH!!!

BOOOM

STEAMWORKS MEDALLION

Great Pumpkin Island

DIFFICULTY: EASY

SYNOPSIS: EVERY HALLOWEEN, KIDS EVERYWHERE WATCH *IT'S THE GREAT PUMPKIN, CHARLIE BROWN*. IN THIS CLASSIC TV SPECIAL, CHARLIE BROWN GOES TRICK-OR-TREATING, LINUS WAITS UP ALL NIGHT FOR THE GREAT PUMPKIN, AND SNOOPY BATTLES THE RED BARON. WHEN YOU VISIT THIS ISLAND, YOU BECOME A PART OF CHARLIE BROWN'S WORLD AND GET TO DO ALL OF THESE THINGS—AND MORE—WITH YOUR FAVORITE PEANUTS CHARACTERS.

FIRST STOP: MAIN STREET

The brightly colored leaves on the ground are a signal that it's fall here on Great Pumpkin Island. Head left after you land and you'll find Snoopy's Doghouse, but he's just chilling there right now. Head right, and you'll pass the Flying Ace Café, a multi-player room. Keep going and you'll run into Charlie Brown, who's excited because he got an invitation to a Halloween party that night.

The house behind Charlie Brown is the Van Pelt House—the home of Linus and Lucy. Nobody's home at the moment. Go back outside and talk to Pigpen. He's sad because he needs a Trick-or-Treat Bag to hold his candy. The next house is Violet's house. Go inside and she'll tell you that you'll need an invitation and a costume if you want to come to her party, too.

If you keep heading right on Main Street you'll come to the Peanuts Store, where you can watch a scene from the Great Pumpkin movie. That's the last stop on Main Street.

THE PUMPKIN PATCH

To the right of Main Street is the Pumpkin Patch. There you'll meet Linus and Lucy. Lucy wants Linus to find the heaviest pumpkin in the patch, and he'll ask for your help. If you accept, you'll have a short time to figure out which pumpkin is heaviest. Start by putting two pumpkins on the seesaw; the heavier pumpkin will hit the ground. Keep dragging one pumpkin at a time onto the other seat on the seesaw. When you've tested them all, drag the pumpkin on the bottom of the seesaw to Lucy.

Lucy is pleased, but she has another challenge for you. You need to push the heavy pumpkin back to the Van Pelt House without breaking it. You'll have to go up and down hills, over bunnies popping out of holes, and past a busy swing set. If the pumpkin breaks, you can start over again. Don't give up!

THE PUMPKIN CHALLENGE

GETTING THE PUMPKIN TO LUCY'S HOUSE IN ONE PIECE ISN'T EASY. HERE ARE SOME TIPS THAT MIGHT HELP:

1. YOU'LL START OUT BY GOING OVER TWO SMALL HILLS. THE PUMPKIN WILL ROLL AWAY FROM YOU AND ROLL OVER A CLIFF. WHEN YOU GET TO THE SECOND HILL, JUMP OVER THE PUMPKIN. IF YOU LAND ON THE EDGE OF THE CLIFF BEFORE THE PUMPKIN DOES, YOU CAN STOP IT.
2. TAKE THE BUNNY HILLS SLOWLY, ONE AT A TIME. WAIT UNTIL EACH BUNNY HEAD DISAPPEARS BEFORE YOU PUSH THE PUMPKIN OVER THE HOLE.
3. IT'S EASY FOR THE PUMPKIN TO GET STUCK IN THE LOG BRIDGE. TAKE A RUNNING START TO GET YOUR PUMPKIN ROLLING QUICKLY SO IT WILL MAKE IT THROUGH TO THE OTHER SIDE. THEN HOP ON THE LOG BRIDGE AS FAST AS YOU CAN TO MEET THE PUMPKIN WHEN IT COMES OUT—OTHERWISE, IT MAY ROLL BACK INTO THE LOG.
4. STOP WHEN YOU GET TO THE SWING SET. WHEN VIOLET SWINGS BACK, QUICKLY ROLL THE PUMPKIN FORWARD, AND YOU'LL GET PAST THE OTHER TWO SWINGS.

THE VAN PELT HOUSE

Linus is grateful that you got the pumpkin to his house in one piece, so he gives you his Trick-or-Treat Bag. Go outside and give the bag to Pigpen. He'll give you a lemon-flavored Sucker—Linus's favorite. Bring the Sucker back inside and Linus will give you his invitation to Violet's party. Before you leave, take the Pen off of Linus's desk.

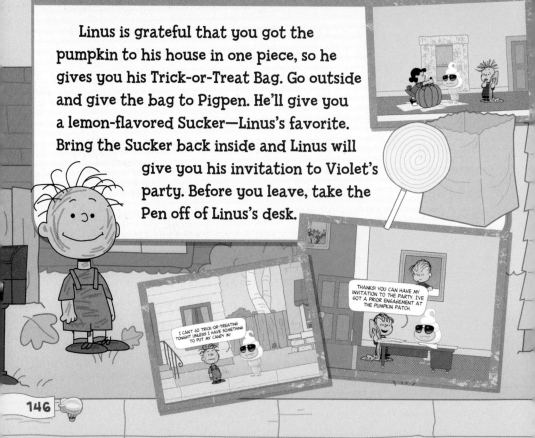

I CAN'T GO TRICK-OR-TREATING TONIGHT UNLESS I HAVE SOMETHING TO PUT MY CANDY IN!

THANKS! YOU CAN HAVE MY INVITATION TO THE PARTY. I'VE GOT A PRIOR ENGAGEMENT AT THE PUMPKIN PATCH.

FUN WITH SNOOPY

Leave the house and head left to Snoopy's Doghouse. You'll find Snoopy and Charlie Brown there. Charlie Brown asks Snoopy to help put falling leaves into a leaf pile. Now you'll play a mini-challenge as Snoopy. Use your mouse to move Snoopy left and right. Click to make Snoopy blow on the leaves, suspending them in the air. Once you move five leaves into the pile, the challenge is over.

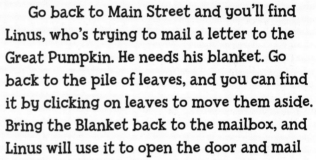

Go back to Main Street and you'll find Linus, who's trying to mail a letter to the Great Pumpkin. He needs his blanket. Go back to the pile of leaves, and you can find it by clicking on leaves to move them aside. Bring the Blanket back to the mailbox, and Linus will use it to open the door and mail his letter. He asks you to wait in the Pumpkin Patch with him, but you tell him you'd rather go to the party.

You have your Party Invitation, but you still need a costume (and regular Poptropica costumes just won't cut it here). Go back toward Snoopy's Doghouse and you'll find Lucy and Charlie Brown arguing. Lucy wants to hold the Football so Charlie Brown can kick it, but he's afraid she's going to move it away at the last second, like always. Lucy says she'll sign a document saying she won't do it, but Charlie Brown doesn't have a pen. Go to your items and click on the Pen you found on Linus's desk.

Lucy and Charlie Brown will give you the Football. Take the Football to Snoopy's Doghouse and use it to knock Snoopy's flight cap out of

the tree. Now you can play with Snoopy as he imagines he is a World War I pilot fighting the evil Red Baron. Use your mouse to move Snoopy's Doghouse through the sky. Avoid the Red Baron's plane and the missiles he drops. If you can last for one minute, you win the challenge.

By now it's dark out, and you and Snoopy must get through a bombed-out village to safety. A searchlight shines down from the sky, and you have to avoid it. Run from hiding spot to hiding spot, timing your moves to avoid the beam.

Once you make it through the village, you'll find a scarecrow wearing a Halloween Mask. You've found the costume you need to get into Violet's party! Put on the Mask and go inside the next house.

TIP:
When you get to the first house, jump to the roof and hide behind the chimney.

PARTY TIME

Inside Violet's party, you'll be asked to play four games. First you'll have to bob for apples and draw a jack-o'-lantern face. Then you'll play "Pin the Face on the Pumpkin." A pumpkin face will move around on your screen, and then the screen goes black. You have to put the stem, eyes, nose, and mouth where you think they belong.

In the last game, you need to play notes on Schroeder's piano. The notes will scroll down the screen, and you have to hit the

TIP:
When the pumpkin stops moving, touch your finger to the screen before it disappears to keep track of its location. Then it's easier to remember where to put all the pieces.

piano keys when the notes hit. A blue bar on the bottom right will show you how well you're doing.

TRICK OR TREAT

When the games are finished, it's time to go trick-or-treating. The gang will head to the Pumpkin Patch first to convince Linus to go with them, but he won't budge. Sally agrees to stay with him.

Follow the trick-or-treaters from house to house. You'll have to knock on each door. Candy will come flying out. Jump up to catch one piece of candy. You need to get a different piece from each house to fill your bag. If you succeed, you'll get a Bag of Candy added to your Inventory.

IT'S THE GREAT PUMPKIN— OR IS IT?

Go back to the Pumpkin Patch and give Sally your Bag of Candy. You will hear something rustling among the pumpkin vines. Is it the Great Pumpkin? (We won't spoil the ending for you, but if you've seen the special, you already know.)

Time passes, and Lucy shows up in the middle of the night. Linus is sound asleep, wrapped in his blanket. Lucy thanks you for taking care of her brother and gives you an Island Medallion.

GREAT PUMPKIN MEDALLION

cryptids ISLAND

DIFFICULTY: HARD

SYNOPSIS: ECCENTRIC RICH GUY HAROLD MEWS IS OBSESSED WITH MORE THAN MONEY—HE WANTS TO PROVE THE EXISTENCE OF CRYPTIDS, LEGENDARY CREATURES SUCH AS BIGFOOT AND THE LOCH NESS MONSTER. HE'S OFFERING ONE MILLION DOLLARS TO THE PERSON WHO CAN BRING HIM DEFINITE PROOF. TO GET THE PROOF AND WIN THE PRIZE, YOU'LL HAVE TO FLY TO FARAWAY LANDS, EXPLORE CREEPY LOCATIONS, AND AVOID GRETCHEN GRIMLOCK, A VILLAINOUS FORTUNE HUNTER WHO WILL DO ANYTHING TO BEAT YOU.

FIRST STOP: MAIN STREET

Land in this pleasant seaside village and you'll find the place crawling with fortune hunters who are all vying for Harold Mews's million-dollar prize. Many people are looking for a way off of the Island to go hunt for cryptids.

On Main Street you'll find the General Store, Kitty's Kites, and Bert's Bed & Breakfast, a multi-player room. You can't buy anything in the General Store without money. But the kite store has a try-it-before-you-buy-it policy. The only thing you can't try is the Kitesurfer X250. The clerk tells you it needs stronger string, and they're all out of the stronger string.

CLIFF PARK

You might as well take your kite out for a spin in Cliff Park. It's very windy there. You'll see a few people trying to leave the Island in hot-air balloons. One girl is using a hang glider and asks you for a push. If you climb up to the roof of the house overlooking the cliff, you'll find a balloonist attached to the house by a rope. He'll ask you to cut him loose but you don't have the right tools for the job.

CLIFF MANSIONS

Seeing all those fortune hunters taking off inspires you to try to find this Harold Mews and see about getting the reward for yourself. Leave Cliff Park, go back to Main Street, and walk toward the right until you get to a bunch of mansions. There are gates blocking your way in. You'll meet a thirsty Gardener who complains about the heat. You'd like to help him, and you know they sell drinks at the General Store, but right now you're broke.

I'M SO THIRSTY. IT'S HOTTER THAN THE JERSEY DEVIL'S BREATH OUT HERE!

Keep going right and you'll run into two more fortune hunters. Look up and you'll see a five-dollar bill fluttering in the tree branches. Jump up to get it. If you keep going right, you'll get to Mews Mansion, but there's still no way to get in.

You might as well help out the Gardener. Go back to the General Store and click on your five-dollar bill to buy a Sports Drink. Bring it to the Gardener and offer it to him. He will ask you to hold his Garden Shears while he runs an errand.

GRETCHEN GRIMLOCK ATTACKS!

The Shears remind you of that balloonist who can't get off the ground. Use the Shears to cut the rope for him, and you can get the Nylon Rope. Didn't the kite-store clerk say you needed strong rope for that kite-surfing kite?

Go back to the kite shop, click on the Rope in your Items, and you will be able to get the Kitesurfer X250. Go back to Cliff Park and head all the way to the left. Jump off the rocks into the ocean, and use the kite. You'll be bopping across the waves when a purple speedboat appears out of nowhere and a woman with streaked purple hair sets fire to your kite! She'll warn you to give up—the prize money is hers. Luckily, a helicopter will come to your rescue.

INSIDE THE MEWS MANSION

You'll wake up in a bed inside the Mews Mansion. Harold Mews is sitting next to you. He'll tell you that the woman who attacked you was Gretchen Grimlock, a ruthless fortune hunter. He'll ask you to join him in the foyer when you're feeling better.

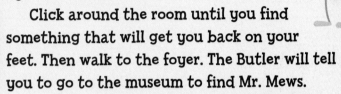

Click around the room until you find something that will get you back on your feet. Then walk to the foyer. The Butler will tell you to go to the museum to find Mr. Mews.

The museum turns out to be a Cryptids Museum, with displays of five legendary creatures. One of the displays contains a live giant squid! That's one cryptid whose existence has been confirmed. The others are all unproven: Bigfoot, the Loch Ness Monster, the Jersey Devil, and the Chupacabra. Click on the green control button at each display to hear about them. You may learn something that will help you later in the game.

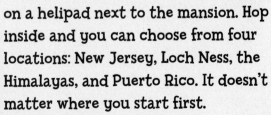

After you check out all five displays, Harold Mews appears and tells you he thinks you have what it takes to find him the proof he so desperately wants. He offers you the use of his private helicopter and asks you to bring your evidence back to the museum after you find it.

Go outside, make a right, and you'll find the helicopter

on a helipad next to the mansion. Hop inside and you can choose from four locations: New Jersey, Loch Ness, the Himalayas, and Puerto Rico. It doesn't matter where you start first.

THE DEEP WATERS OF LOCH NESS

If you fly to this Scottish town next, you'll find a bunch of tourists on the dock, trying to spot the Loch Ness Monster. Down by the water there is a man offering a submarine tour of the loch (a sea's lakelike extension into land), and another offering a rowboat tour. But you need a ticket for each one, and the ticket booth seems to be closed.

Walk up the hill to the Castle and you'll find a viewer you can look through to see what's in the loch. Head back down the hill and make your way to the right toward the Nessie Pub. You'll find a man whose vehicle is stuck in the mud. To help him, you need to click on his tire and let the air out by moving your cursor in a circular motion around the air intake. He'll thank you for your help by giving you a Rugged Camera.

Keep going to the Pub and you'll see some Matches that you can pick up. You'll talk to two local men—one believes in Nessie, and the other doesn't. Talk to the man with the red mustache and he'll challenge you to a game of darts. He'll give you a set of Ratty Darts so you can play.

It may take a few tries to get the hang of the game, but if you keep at it, you will beat him. When you win, you'll get a set of Osprey Darts as well as a Rowboat Ticket. Head back to the dock and take the rowboat tour. You'll see something strange in the water, but you can't get close enough. Use your camera to take a picture.

It's your first piece of evidence! Fly back to the Mews Mansion and go down to the lab.

TRY, TRY AGAIN

Harold Mews will examine the photo and tell you that the rowboat tour guide has tricked you. Head back to Loch Ness and try again.

Confront the rowboat tour guide and he'll hurry off, leaving you his boat. The submarine tour looks promising but you still need a ticket. Go back to the pub and talk to the two men you met before. The Nessie believer will tell you he saw the monster while he was scuba diving near Cherry Island. His friend says that if you beat him in darts, he'll give you a Submarine Ticket.

You'll find that the Osprey Darts make playing the game a little easier. Once you beat the man in the white cap, he'll give you the ticket. Go back to the submarine tour guide and he'll take you to Cherry Island. You see something that looks just like the monster under the water! Use your camera to get the Loch Ness Monster photo.

Take your photo back to the Pub and show it to the two men. The man in the white cap laughs and points to a news article on the wall. The monster you've just seen is actually a movie prop. You're starting to wonder if it's even possible to get proof of Nessie. But the man doesn't want any hard feelings between you, so he gives you Peregrine Feathered Darts as a souvenir.

The man with the red mustache challenges you again and promises you a great prize if you win. Now that you've got top-notch darts, you beat him easily. But he's a sore loser and won't live up to his promise. Luckily, the pub owner feels bad for you and gives you a Pennywhistle.

He says it's supposed to summon Nessie when it's played.

You might as well give it one more try. Head out on the rowboat again, go all the way to the cove, and use the whistle. You might be surprised at what you find. Take a photo and bring it back to the lab to show Mews. This time, he's pleased with what he sees.

THE FROZEN LAND OF THE YETI

The Himalayas in Nepal are said to be the home of the Yeti. In the museum, you learned that the monks here keep a Yeti scalp in their monastery. That would be terrific evidence to bring back to Mews! But to get to the monastery, you'll have to climb up the snowy mountain. Talk to the people you see until you find a Sherpa Guide who will help you.

Traveling up the mountain isn't easy. You and the Sherpa are connected by a strong rope. You need to climb up the mountain and click on the metal rings you see. Click on a ring to attach the rope and the Sherpa will follow you. If you fall, just climb back up the rope and keep going.

TIP: There are strong winds on the mountain. When the wind whips up, stay still or it will blow you off the mountain. Wait until the wind dies down to move again.

When you get to the top of the mountain, go left and the monks will greet you. Inside the monastery you will see a glass case that holds what is supposed to be a

Yeti scalp. The monks inside won't give it to you, but one of them will give you an Unlit Camping Lantern to help you on your journey.

Leave the monastery and climb up to the roof of the temple. If you beat the monk there at a simple game, he will let you pass. Keep going and you'll find a big footprint. Could this be a Yeti's footprint? If you got the camera in Loch Ness, you can take a Photo of the Snow Track to bring back to Harold Mews.

Possible Yeti track?

LAND OF THE CHUPACABRA

It's time to explore a new location. If you head to Puerto Rico next, you'll land on a small, dusty farm. You'll meet a farmer who complains that the fortune hunters are scaring off his goats. He will lend you his jeep if you deliver some seeds to his brother.

When you ride in the jeep, you'll be seeing the action from a bird's-eye view. Use the map in the corner of the screen to chart your course. Head north until you reach the farmer's brother's farm.

He will tell you that the Chupacabra raided his chicken coop last night. Examine the coop and you can collect a sample of Unidentified Fur. Could this be the proof you need?

Fly back to the lab and test it. It's not Chupacabra fur—but you can't give up now. Borrow the farmer's

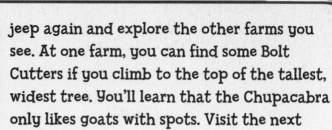

jeep again and explore the other farms you see. At one farm, you can find some Bolt Cutters if you climb to the top of the tallest, widest tree. You'll learn that the Chupacabra only likes goats with spots. Visit the next farm and that farmer will tell you the Chupacabra only attacks goats in groups of three or more.

If you talk to the farmer's brother he'll tell you his friend saw the Chupacabra on an outcropping overlooking the river. Drive northwest in search of the outcropping, and you'll see goats roaming the fields. You need to herd three spotted goats onto a patch of dark green grass using your jeep. You can herd them one at a time—once they're on the grass, they won't move.

Once you have the three goats, you can exit the jeep. You realize you have the bait, but you need a trap. Go back to the first farmer, the one who lent you the jeep, to see if he can help.

After you talk to him, he will meet you by the three spotted goats. He'll set a trap—and it works! Something is inside the wooden crate. He'll ask you to push it on the truck when . . . something really startling happens. You'll survive, and you'll have a Chupacabra Tooth to remind you of your adventure. Bring the tooth back to Harold Mews in the lab.

TAKE A REST IN NEW JERSEY

When you land the helicopter, you'll find yourself at a gas station and rest stop off a New Jersey highway. It's dark out, and there's not much sign of life. Head to the rest stop and you'll find the hang glider you helped earlier stuck in a tree. Use the Garden Shears to free her, and she'll give you a message.

You'll find a dumpster just outside the rest stop, but it's locked. If you got the Bolt Cutters in Puerto Rico you can open it up. Dig through the trash and you'll find something interesting at the bottom—an old bathroom stall door with what looks like directions written on it. Pick up the door and head inside.

Right, left
Over the cleft

Left, right
Into the night

Right, right
Shudder with fright

Left, left
Mother bereft

The Maintenance Man will tell you that he's been putting new doors on the stalls. You'll see another door with directions on it. Put the two doors together and you'll get the Bathroom Door Message. It appears to be directing you somewhere—could it be to the location of the Jersey Devil?

"I GREW UP IN NEW JERSEY, SO I'VE HEARD LEGENDS OF THE JERSEY DEVIL SINCE I WAS A KID."
—MEDUSA, AKA TRACEY WEST

INTO THE DARK WOODS

Leave the Rest Stop and you'll see a motorcycle. Hop on it and you'll ride it into the woods. Once again, you'll get a bird's-eye view of the path as you maneuver your bike through the trees. Follow the directions from the bathroom stall doors *exactly* and you'll come to an intersection. Stop the motorcycle and look around.

It's too dark to see anything, but if you have the Unlit Camping Lantern and matches, you can light your way. Follow the path through the spooky gate to an old stone house. This is Shroud House, the legendary birthplace of the Jersey Devil. Go to the second floor, and you'll hear a sound in the attic. Push the dresser to the left so you can jump upstairs. In the attic you'll find the Grappling Hook.

Head back downstairs and you'll see something surprising in the window. It's time to give chase! Run outside to see if you can catch it. You may find the creature's nest, but you'll need the Grappling Hook to get to it. There's some key evidence in there—broken egg shells. Bring them back to the lab to see if you can confirm the legend of the Jersey Devil.

THE BATTLE WITH GRETCHEN GRIMLOCK

Once you have delivered the Broken Egg Shells, Chupacabra Tooth, Loch Ness Monster Photo, and the Photo of Snow Track to Harold Mews, he'll tell you some exciting news. There's been a Bigfoot sighting in the Pacific Northwest! Fly there in your helicopter and see if you can spot Bigfoot on the ground. When you do, follow him to see if you can find where he lives.

HINT:
Bigfoot's cave is in a group of large rocks in the north.

When you find him, you'll contact Harold Mews. Your transmission will be interrupted by Gretchen Grimlock, who has zeroed in on your location. She wants Bigfoot for herself so she can make millions parading him around the world. She grabs Bigfoot and takes off in her helicopter, which is bigger than yours.

Chase her until you catch up to her. Then you'll jump out of your helicopter onto Bigfoot's cage, which is hanging from the helicopter by a rope. Then you'll have to find a way to bring down Gretchen's helicopter and free Bigfoot at the same time.

HINT:
Detaching the gas tank from Gretchen's helicopter is a surefire way to stop her—if you can get to it.

If you succeed, Harold Mews will give you an Island Medallion—and you'll find a way to use your million-dollar reward to help Bigfoot.

GRETCHEN WON'T GET FAR WITHOUT FUEL!

CRYPTIDS MEDALLION

WILD WEST island

DIFFICULTY: HARD

SYNOPSIS: BAD GUY EL MUSTACHIO GRANDE AND HIS NO-GOOD GRANDE GANG ARE RUNNING WILD IN THESE WESTERN TOWNS. THEY'RE SO ROTTEN THEY'D STEAL A BOTTLE RIGHT OUT OF A BABY'S HANDS. THE MARSHAL OF DUSTY GULCH HAS GIVEN UP ON TRYING TO CAPTURE THESE BANK-ROBBING BANDITS. ARE YOU BRAVE ENOUGH TO STEP INTO THE MARSHAL'S BOOTS AND TAKE DOWN THE GANG YOURSELF?

Poptropica

FIRST STOP: MAIN STREET

Main Street on this Island is in the town of Dusty Gulch. The first thing you'll see is an exhausted Pony Express Rider on top of her horse. She's got to deliver a letter to Marshal Flint Taylor in Diamond Plains. You can offer to help, but she'll tell you you'll need your own steed (a horse).

Head down the street and you'll pass the Dusty Gulch Hotel, a common room. That's where you'll spot the first "Wanted" poster for El Mustachio Grande. Talk to the man hanging it up, and he'll tell you all about Mustachio and his gang of bandits.

YOU? YOU'RE NOT WORTH WASTING A PLATE ON, WHIPPERSNAPPER.

Next to the hotel you'll find a Photography Stand, which advertises free photo portraits. But when you ask for one, the photographer will tell you that you're not worth it. You'll have to come back when you make something of yourself. Now how exactly are you supposed to do that?

Keep going and you'll come to the Trading Post. You'll find the owner on the second floor wearing a coonskin cap. He's willing to trade with you—but you don't have anything to trade right now.

To the right of the Trading Post you'll find Rusty's Ranch, where a rancher is trying to tame a wild horse named Elmer. He tells you if you can do it, the horse is yours. If you succeed, you not only get Elmer, but a Horse Whistle that you can use to call Elmer to you if you ever get separated.

Now that you've got your own steed, you can go back and help that exhausted Pony Express Rider.

ANY TIME YOU TWO GET SEPARATED, GIVE THIS WHISTLE A TOOT AND HE'LL COME A-RUNNIN'.

THANKS. YOU'LL FIND MARSHAL TAYLOR IN DIAMOND PLAINS.

The Pony Express Rider will give you the Letter to the Marshal that you need to deliver to Marshal Taylor in Diamond Plains. Go left to leave town, and you'll find yourself looking down on you and your horse on the wide open plains from a bird's-eye view. Click on the map on the top right so you can plot your course to Diamond Plains. See that little white dot that's moving? That's you!

Click on the yellow star to enter Diamond Plains. The first place you'll see is the Marshal's Office. You can go inside, but you won't find the marshal there—his deputy will tell you to look for him in the saloon.

On the way there you'll pass the Clock Tower, where the bearded man will tell you he's fixing it all by himself. There's nothing you can do to help him now, so go right to Ruby's Root Beer Saloon. You can look around, but you won't find the marshal right away. You will find two men playing a gum-chewing game, Spit-n-Time. If you can beat one of them, they'll tell you where to find the marshal.

When you win, you'll be directed to the marshal, who's snoozing at one of the tables. You can show him the letter, which is from the manager of McGready's Bank in Rock Ridge. He's got word that El Mustachio and the gang are going to rob the bank, and he wants the marshal's help.

TIP:
Watch the angle and intensity your opponent uses and try to match that when it's your turn.

But Marshal Taylor is done with fighting bad guys. He might be defeated, but you're just getting started. Ask him, and he'll give you his Marshal's Badge.

THERE'S A NEW MARSHAL IN TOWN!

Ride proudly back to the Marshal's Office with your Badge. The deputy will tell you that you need an Official Marshal's Portrait before you can do the marshal's job. Luckily, you remember the photographer back in Dusty Gulch. Now that you've made something of yourself, he's *got* to take your photo!

Ride out to Dusty Gulch, get your portrait taken, and then bring it back to the Marshal's Office. Now that you're official, the deputy will give you a Pea Shooter.

Suddenly, the office begins to rumble. It's a jailbreak! Members of the Grande Gang have blasted through the walls of the jail cell and sprung one of their own from behind bars. They take off on horseback—and you've got to follow them.

The gang gets away before you can catch them. But you never know where they'll show up next. Now is a good time to check out the other towns on the map and see how things are doing there.

TEST YOUR SKILLS IN DOS CACTOS

If you enter Dos Cactos from the west, the first thing you'll see is the Shooting Contest. Head inside to test your skills with the Pea Shooter in a shooting gallery. You'll face five opponents, each one better than the last: the Man with

No Name, the Young Kid, the Gunslinger, the Old Gunslinger, and Miss Annie Oakley. If you beat them all, you'll get the Spud Gun, which packs a powerful potato punch.

LITTLE SURE SHOT

ANNIE OAKLEY WAS A REAL SHARPSHOOTER WHO WAS BORN IN 1860 IN OHIO. SHE LEARNED HOW TO SHOOT WHEN SHE WAS A YOUNG GIRL. WHEN SHE WAS JUST FIFTEEN, SHE COMPETED AGAINST FRANK BUTLER, A SHARPSHOOTING CHAMPION, AND BEAT HIM! FRANK AND ANNIE LATER MARRIED AND SHE JOINED HIS TRAVELING SHOW. SHE SOON BECAME FAMOUS ALL OVER THE WORLD FOR HER AMAZING SKILLS. HER AIM WAS SO ACCURATE THAT SHE COULD SHOOT OUT THE FLAME ON A CANDLE WITHOUT HITTING THE CANDLE AT ALL!

When you're done with the contest, you might as well explore Dos Cactos. Head right and climb up the rocks to get

to the Four Aces Casino. Go upstairs and a man wearing glasses will invite you to play a game of Slapjack. You and three opponents will take turns flipping over a card and putting it on a pile in the middle of the table. If

someone puts a jack on the pile, try to slap it as quickly as you can. If you're the first one to slap it, you get it and all the cards underneath it.

TIP:
Keep your cursor over the pile of cards when it's not your turn so that you can slap a jack when you see it. But be careful—some of the players will try to trick you by only putting the card part of the way on the pile. Be patient and wait until the card is all the way on. Then slap away!

The player who ends up with all of the cards wins the game.

If you win the game, the man who challenged you will give you a Map to Gold. You can follow the Map to where gold is located, but you can't dig without a Gold Pan. You may remember seeing one at the Trading Post, but don't head there yet—you need something to trade with, and, as the new marshal, you're going to need your Pea Shooter and Spud Shooter. Your search for gold will have to wait for now.

Before you leave Dos Cactos, check out the Train Station. By now you've probably figured out that the trains aren't running. But the most interesting thing you'll find here is a dude with an enormous head! He'll tell you that R.J. Earl in Rock Ridge sold him a tonic that was supposed to make him smart, but gave him a big cranium instead. He says there's a Blue Tulip that can cure him, and it grows in dark places.

ROUND 'EM UP IN
ROCK RIDGE

There are no dark places in Dos Cactos, so saddle up and ride on out to the last town on the Map, Rock Ridge. If you enter from the west, you'll encounter a Cattle Driver who looks distressed. She'll tell you she's lost one of her calves and gives you a Lasso so you can go catch her.

IF YOU CAN FIND MY CALF, PLEASE TAKE HER TO MY RANCH JUST WEST OF HERE! THEN COME BACK AND TALK TO ME.

Ride out into the desert and follow the hoof prints you see in the sand. When you get close enough to the missing calf, use the Lasso in your Items. You have the Lasso automatically, but to make it appear, you'll have to press the spacebar. Press the spacebar once to twirl the Lasso. Once the lasso is over your target, press the spacebar to throw it. If your aim is right, you'll wrangle the cattle.

NOW DON'T GO WANDERIN' OFF AGAIN!

When you've got the calf, take her to the Ranch, which you can find on the bottom of the map. Once she's safely in the corral, she won't get out again. Then go back to the Cattle Driver in Rock Ridge and tell her you've succeeded. She will give you an Old Saddle as a reward.

If you talk to her again, she'll offer you an extra challenge: Round up five more calves and bring them to the Ranch and she'll give you another reward. You can choose to do this now or come back later. If you succeed, you'll win the Rattlesnake Wrangler Costume.

PANNING FOR GOLD

Now that you have the Old Saddle, you have something you can trade at the Trading Post. Ride back to Dusty Gulch and the owner of the Trading Post will offer you an Oilcan or Gold Pan for the saddle. Take the Gold Pan for now—you can always get the Oilcan later.

Now that you have the Map to Gold and the Gold Pan, you are ready to start treasure hunting. Leave town and look at the Map. You'll see that there's a new

gold star on the Map—on a place where two rivers meet. Ride Elmer to the spot. Then click the star on the Map to use the Gold Pan to search for a Gold Nugget.

MEET THE SNAKE
OIL SALESMAN

You're probably itching to spend that Gold Nugget, but so far, you haven't seen anything you can buy. This is a good time to head back to Rock Ridge because you haven't finished exploring there yet.

Just past the Cattle Driver you'll see a colorful wagon with a sign on it: "R.J. Earl's Genuine Elixirs, Fixers and Magnificent Mixers." You've been seeing signs for R.J. Earl's goods all

over the Island. And the dude with the big head said his large cranium is R.J. Earl's fault. What's this guy up to?

As you approach, you'll see a man buying one of Earl's tonics. When he drinks it, he turns invisible! You're curious. An invisibility tonic could come in handy. Talk to R.J. Earl, though, and he'll say you don't have enough money to buy his goods. But he's wrong, of course. You've got a Gold Nugget! Show it to him and he'll sell you one of every one of R.J. Earl's Tonics.

THIS WAS SUPPOSED TO MAKE ME FEEL LIGHTER THAN AIR, NOT LOOK LIKE AIR!

To use a tonic, click on the item's card. Click on one of the colored circles. Then click "use." There are five to choose from:

Don't panic if you don't like the effect of a tonic—it wears off after a short time.

ALL NATURAL NOGGIN: MAKES YOUR HEAD HUGE

BEARD BREW: MAKES YOU SPROUT AN AWESOME BEARD

CONCENTRATION CARBONATE: MAKES YOU REACT FASTER AND MORE ACCURATELY

SHRINKING SODA: MAKES YOU SMALL

TRANSPARENCY TONIC: MAKES YOU INVISIBLE

R.J. EARL: A CURIOUS CHARACTER

THE GUY WITH THE BIG HEAD CALLS R.J. EARL A "SNAKE OIL SALESMAN." THAT'S A TERM THAT BECAME POPULAR IN OLD WESTERN MOVIES. IT REFERS TO A KIND OF SALESMAN WHO WOULD SELL MEDICINES THAT WERE SUPPOSED TO DO INCREDIBLE THINGS, LIKE MAKE YOU INSTANTLY GROW TALLER OR BECOME SMARTER. BUT HIS MEDICINES REALLY DIDN'T DO THOSE THINGS AT ALL. IN FACT, THEY WERE OFTEN DANGEROUS TO A PERSON'S HEALTH.

NOT YOURS-MINE!

Next to R.J. Earl's wagon is McGready's Bank. Remember that letter that you delivered to Marshal Taylor? This is the bank that's in trouble. The bank manager is nervous—he's afraid the Grande Gang will strike at any moment. You haven't seen any sign of them since the jailbreak. Maybe you'd better go looking for them.

If you climb up the ladder next to the bank you'll come to the Rock Ridge Train Station. There's no train running. Go right and you'll see a sign for the Mine. Hey, that's a dark place! Maybe you can find the Blue Tulip that the man with the big head is looking for.

The door to the mine is locked, and there's a strange message about a canary on it. Look around and you'll see a yellow canary with a key around its neck. Use your Pea Shooter to shoot the key off of the bird's neck. Then enter the Mine, but watch out! There are rocks falling from the ceiling.

Hop in a mine cart and take a ride on the tracks. You'll have to dodge bats and falling rocks and watch out for broken tracks. You'll also need to shoot the switches in order to keep the track intact. If you make it to the end, you'll be able to pick the Blue Tulip. After you get it, climb the rope to leave the Mine.

GET THOSE GEARS MOVING

THANK YOU. HERE, TAKE THIS SCRAP I FOUND! SEEMS LIKE IT COULD BE WORTH SOMETHING.

Ride to Dos Cactos to deliver the Blue Tulip to the man with the big noggin. (If you've lost track of Elmer, just use your Horse Whistle and he'll come right to you.) To thank you, the man with the big head will give you a piece of the Map to the Hideout—the hideout of the Grande Gang! But you still need to find one more piece of the Map.

As long as you're looking for the Map, you might as well head back to Dusty Gulch and trade in the Gold Pan for the Oilcan. You're done with the pan, and the Oilcan might come in handy.

Then ride to Diamond Plains and go back to the Clock Tower. The guy fixing it up needed some help—maybe if you help him, you'll get a reward. The gears of the clock are high up in the tower, so you'll have to climb up. Push the crates to get to the best spots for jumping. You can also walk across the steel beams. Each of the steel beams is tied to a long rope. To drop a beam, you have to untie the other end of the rope by clicking on it.

When you get to the top, you'll discover that the clock's gears are rusty. Good thing you have that Oilcan! But you don't have enough oil to loosen up every gear. Locate the large silver gear on the bottom and trace the shortest path from it to the next largest silver gear.

TIP:

To oil a gear, place the Oilcan over it and hold down your mouse. The oil will stop flowing automatically once the gear is no longer rusty.

Watch your step

Then use your Oilcan to oil only those gears.

You've fixed the clock! There's no reward from the man fixing the clock tower, but something cool happens—the

train arrives at the station! Hop on board and head to Rock Ridge to check on the bank. Make sure you have the Spud Gun before getting on the train.

THE GREAT TRAIN ROBBERY

Right after the train leaves the station, a bandit on horseback starts shooting at it. It's a member of the Grande Gang! You'll need to scare him off with your Spud Gun. But aiming at a moving man while

you're on a moving train isn't easy. It's a good thing you have R.J. Earl's Tonics. Press the spacebar to use the Concentration Carbonate. You'll improve your speed and accuracy. Each use depletes the amount you have. Once you've run out, you're out unless you restart.

Frighten off the bandits and you'll arrive safely in Rock Ridge. Go to the bank and you'll find the place in ruins. You're too late! The manager will tell you that the gang has already robbed the bank. But they left something behind: It's the missing scrap of the Map to their hideout that you need. Now the secret location is added to your Map. It's time to go rassle up some no-good, thievin' varmints!

SHOOTOUT IN THE HIDEOUT

Ride Elmer out of Rock Ridge and look at your Map. You'll see a new star where the hideout is. Ride up to the hideout and you'll realize that it's heavily guarded by the Grande Gang. There's no way you can get inside without being seen . . . or is there?

Luckily, you've got R.J. Earl's Tonics. Dismount Elmer, take some Transparency Tonic, and hurry inside the hideout before it wears off. Once you're in, you'll need to use your Spud Shooter to force four members of the Grande Gang from their hiding places. Shoot at the objects in the room to flush them out. Then knock out each gang member with a potato punch before they shoot you. You can use the Concentration Tonic here, if you need it.

HINT:

Aim for the bag of money on top of the safe, the wick of the candle, the small barrel of root beer, and the musket on top of the fireplace.

El Mustachio himself is hiding behind a big barrel in the room. Don't waste your potatoes on him because there's no way to get him in the hideout. Avoid him if you can or he'll shoot you.

Once you take out his four gang members, El Mustachio will flee the hideout on horseback. Jump on Elmer and ride after him.

LASSO THE BAD GUY

You'll need to use your Lasso to round up El Mustachio the same way you rounded up those cattle before—except that El Mustachio is must faster and harder to catch than a cow. If you manage to capture him, you'll have to bring him back to Diamond Plains. Once you enter the town, you'll automatically be brought back to Marshal Taylor's office. Marshal Taylor will thank you for putting this bad guy behind bars, and give you an Island Medallion for your trouble.

Wimpy WONDERLAND

DIFFICULTY: EASY

SYNOPSIS: MAYBE YOU'VE READ EVERY SINGLE BOOK IN THE *DIARY OF A WIMPY KID* SERIES BY JEFF KINNEY. MAYBE YOU'VE SEEN BOTH MOVIES TEN TIMES EACH. WELL, NOW, THANKS TO POPTROPICA, YOU CAN ACTUALLY ENTER THE WIMPY WORLD OF GREG HEFFLEY AND HIS FRIENDS! IN WIMPY WONDERLAND, YOU'LL EXPLORE GREG'S TOWN AS YOU HELP HIM FIND HIS MISSING LITTLE BROTHER, MANNY.

FIRST STOP: MAIN STREET

When you jump down from the blimp, you'll find yourself in a snowy wonderland. Greg Heffley is standing on the sidewalk underneath your blimp. Talk to him, and he'll tell you that his little brother, Manny, is missing. He is supposed to be watching Manny while his mom is working. You ask Greg where he saw Manny last, and Greg tells you it was at his house. You can follow Greg to the left to go to the house to look for clues. On the way, you'll pass the Fast Mart, where a bunch of surly teenagers are hanging out.

FOOTPRINTS ON SURREY STREET

Greg will lead you to his house on Surrey Street. He'll tell you that he couldn't find Manny anywhere in the house, and there are no footprints outside to show where he might have gone. You notice that the van of the band Löded

Diper is parked in the driveway, blocking the garage.

Inside, Greg's older brother, Rodrick (the drummer for Löded Diper), is blasting his stereo in his room, and you can't get in there, either. You'll also find that the laundry room is locked, but there are other rooms you can explore.

Go upstairs to find an Address Book in Greg's parents' bedroom. Pick it up because it will come in handy later. Inside Greg's room, you can get a Page from Greg's Journal that gives some clues about the location of his locker. When you get into Manny's room, you'll see that the drawers of his dresser are open, acting like stairs that lead to an open window. *Aha!* That must be how Manny escaped.

FUN FACT:
Greg's Journal mentions Holly Hills, his secret crush, and, according to Greg, "the fourth-prettiest girl in the school."

Climb out the window and you'll see Manny's footprints on the rooftop! Follow them off the roof and through the snow

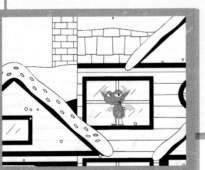

and you'll see Greg's friend Rowley, who complains that somebody stole his Rumble Bike. Suddenly, you see a kid on a Rumble Bike race by you. It's Manny! Chase after him.

Chase Manny back to Main Street. You'll lose him when you get to the Fast Mart, but you'll see that he's ditched the Rumble Bike. Pick it up and keep heading right.

You'll see Manny again, and this time he'll try to escape by jumping into the trees. Follow him. When he jumps down near the Gazebo, he'll destroy a snowman made by a little kid. Pick up the Carrot that was the snowman's nose and keep going.

As you chase Manny you'll pass the Wimpy Kid Store, where you can learn more about the *Diary of a Wimpy Kid* books and movies. The Photo Gallery is a common room where you can check out cool Wimpy Kid art while you battle other players. But you don't have time for any of that now. You've got to catch Manny!

Manny will run to the school and jump up on the window ledges until he gets to a window and climbs in. You can follow him, but you can't jump to the window like Manny did. Hmm . . . there's got to be another way in, right?

Did You Know?:

The first *Diary of a Wimpy Kid* book was published on April 1, 2007.

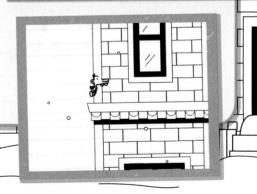

You can check all the other windows, but none will be open. Back on the sidewalk, you'll see that school is closed because of a snow day, and the front door is locked. Looks like that one open window is your only option.

If you walk right, you'll find that a garbage can is blocking your path. If you push it out of the way, it will slide onto the bottom of the seesaw. This gives you an idea. You can use the seesaw to get the garbage can onto the ledge above you, and then you can use the garbage can to get to the open window. You can try jumping on the right side of the seesaw, but it's not enough to get the garbage can as high as you need it. Good thing there's a tall evergreen tree you can climb.

9, 37, 15

As you climb the tree, you'll spot a Scrap of Paper with some numbers on it on one of the branches. You'll definitely need to grab that. Then climb about three-quarters of the way up the tree and jump down onto the seesaw. If you do this just right, the garbage can will fly straight up and land on the ledge.

TIP:

Make sure your cursor arrow is green when you jump to ensure that you don't land short of the seesaw.

Jump up on the ledge and push the garbage can to the left. Then use it to jump to the open window on the highest level. Good job. You're in!

As soon as you jump into the second floor hallway, you'll see Manny. Chase him down the stairs, and he'll run right out the front door. You might be tempted to follow him now, but the little guy is just too speedy and you won't be able to catch him. A better way to spend your time is to look around the school for something useful.

Scroll your mouse over the lockers on the first floor and you'll find that you are able to open one of them—if you have the combination. Luckily you've got that Scrap of Paper from the tree outside. Follow the direction of the arrow to spin the dial and enter the three numbers from the paper. (When you have the right number, it will turn red.) When all three numbers are entered correctly, the locker will open and you can get what's inside: the *Twisted Wizard* Game Guide.

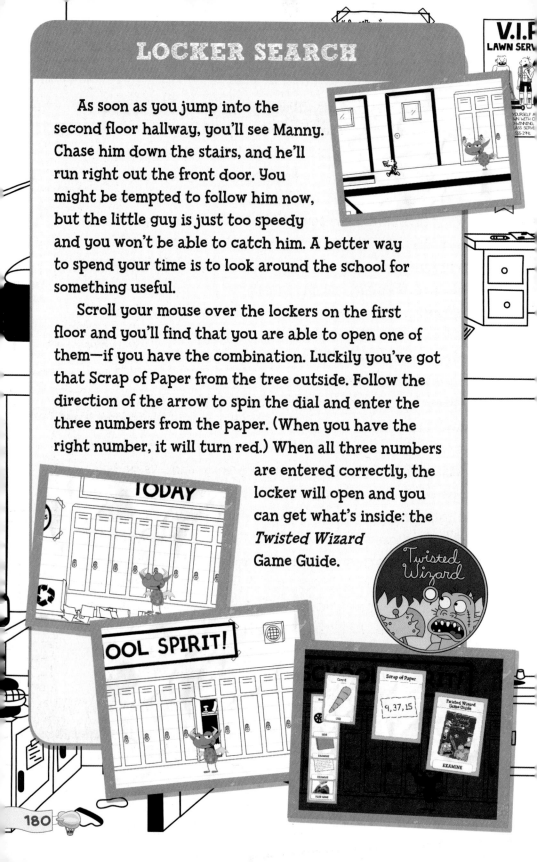

BACK TO SURREY STREET

There's no sign of Manny now, so you might as well head back to Greg's house to see if he's found his little brother. When you get there, you'll see that Greg looks like a zombie—he's been playing the *Twisted Wizard* video game the whole time. Give him the game guide so he can defeat the level and (hopefully) get back to the search. After Greg beats the level, he'll give you the game to return to Rowley.

Along the way to Rowley's house, you pass Fregley's house. There's a snowman on the lawn. Are its eyes following you or are you just seeing things?

When you get to Rowley's house, his grouchy dad won't let you inside. You can see Rowley through the window, looking like a miserable prisoner. There has to be some way to get the game to Rowley. If only you could get his Dad out of the way for a few seconds, you could slip through the front door . . .

To do that, you'll need to jump on the hood of his dad's car. As soon as the alarm goes off, move as fast as you can to the bush to the left of the front door and hide. You'll have to time it just right. If you succeed, you'll be able to enter Rowley's house. Go into his bedroom and give him the *Twisted Wizard* game. He'll be so grateful that he'll give you a Joshie Fan Club Membership Card.

😊 Embarrassing Fact:
Besides Rowley, Joshie's biggest fans are six-year-old girls.

TIP:
You have to click on the bush in order to hide behind it. The "hide" prompt will appear on your cursor over the bush once you've set off the car alarm.

IT'S ALIVE

On the way back to Greg's house you notice the snowman looking at you again, so you click on it, and it will make a muffled noise. Someone is in there under all that snow! Use the Carrot you got from the ruined snowman, and the snowman will ask you to get him out of there. But what can you use to get rid of all that snow?

There might be something in Greg's garage you can use, but you can't get into it as long as the Löded Diper van is there. Rodrick's stereo is so loud that he won't hear you if you knock on the door. There's got to be some way to stop the music.

Head inside Greg's house and look around and you'll notice a circuit breaker in the laundry room, behind the locked door. Use the Joshie card to open the door and then turn off the electricity to Rodrick's basement bedroom. Rodrick will leave his room and go outside.

You might as well check out Rodrick's room while you can. Inside you'll be able to pick up a Dog Dish. Go upstairs and back outside, where you'll see that Rodrick's van is gone. Now you can get inside the garage, where you can pick up a Leaf Blower. It's the perfect tool to get the snow off of whoever's trapped inside the snowman.

Use the Leaf Blower on the snowman and you'll free Fregley, who built his snowman from the inside out. He'll thank you by giving you Fredrick, his Bingo Troll. It's pretty weird, but then again, so is Fregley.

Did You Know?:

Fregley spends every summer in his front yard. Greg is pretty sure it's because Fregley's parents installed an electric fence to keep him in.

GRANDPA'S CLUE

GRAMMA
325 NORTH MAIN STREET

GRAMMIE HEFFLEY
SOUTH STREET, LEISURE TOWERS,
APARTMENT 10A

GRANDPA HEFFLEY
SOUTH STREET, LEISURE TOWERS,
APARTMENT 33C

THE HAPPY FAMILY CLINIC
289 GREEN STREET, SUITE 15B

WHIRLEY STREET BULLIES
WHIRLEY STREET

You might have rescued Fregley, but you still need to find Manny—where should you go? Then you remember the Address Book you found in Greg's house. Examine it and you'll see an apartment number underlined in red—Leisure Towers, 33C, home of Grandpa Heffley.

To get to Leisure Towers, you need to go right, past Main Street and past the school. You can't get in the front door, so hop up and try the windows. It's a long way to 33C, and the elderly residents will try to stop you. When you get to 33C, you can enter the building.

You'll find Grandpa Heffley sleeping in his chair. Wake him up and he'll tell you that he's seen Manny. He'll give you the

TIP:

If there is a person in a window above you, wait until they close the window and then jump quickly to avoid being knocked back down. There seem to be fewer troublemakers in column C, so try to start there when you reach a new level.

details if you join him for lunch. Lunch turns out to be a big bowl of salad, and Grandpa complains about everything as you eat yours. To eat, click the mouse really fast and try to empty the salad bowl before you throw up. If you toss your cookies, you'll have to start all over again.

When you're done, Grandpa will show you a video of Manny on the security camera. It shows him on a motorized scooter, riding back and forth in front of the building. Leave through the door, find the elevator, and take it down to the lobby. When you get outside, you'll see scooter tracks in the snow. Follow them to the right.

Did You Know?:
You can exit on any floor in Leisure Towers and knock on all the doors.

You won't get very far when you run into the Whirley Street Kids! The bullies start throwing snowballs at you. You can't get past them, but before you run away, try to grab the Snow Shovel you see there. It could come in handy on a day like today. You can jump over the flying snowballs to avoid getting hit.

Then go left and resume your search for Manny. You'll see there's a snowplow operator by the plow. He'll complain that his wipers are frozen, and he can't operate his plow without them. Go past the school, down Main Street, and all the way past Rowley's house. You'll come to the Quik-Spin Laundromat. It's so blocked with snow that you can't get inside. It's too bad the snowplow isn't working!

Keep going left and you'll come to Gramma's House. Go inside and Gramma will tell you that Manny showed up earlier, and he seemed to be looking for something. She'll help you find him if you shovel her driveway so she can use her car. Good thing you got that Snow Shovel on Whirley Street! Shovel the snow, but do it fast—if your body temperature drops too low you'll have to start all over.

Once the driveway is clear, Gramma will hop in her car—but instead of helping you look for Manny, she'll tell you she's off to Leisure Towers to play bingo. No fair!

Run after Gramma and enter Leisure Towers where you'll find the speed bingo game about to begin. If you use the lucky Bingo Troll in your Items, then you can play. You'll get three cards. As the bingo balls roll across the top of your screen, move the Troll to stamp the numbers that match the ones on your card. The balls will roll faster and faster as the game moves on, so you'll have to be quick or one of the other players will call *bingo* first.

When you win, you'll get the grand prize, the *Soothing Sounds of Classical Music* CD. Oh well. At least you won!

HELP THE SNOWPLOW DRIVER

You still need to find Manny, and the laundromat is the only place you haven't checked. You know that if the snowplow driver can get his wipers working, he'll be able to plow. So head to the Fast Mart and see if you can get some wiper fluid.

The store has plenty in stock, and the owner says he'll give you some if you can get rid of those teenagers hanging out outside his store. If you talk to them, they'll just tell you to buzz off. Check the Items in your backpack, and you'll see something that might help: the classical music CD you just won. Go inside and use the CD. It will pop into the store's music player. Turn the volume all the way up and the teens will leave in search of better music.

The store owner will reward you with No-Freez Wiper Fluid.

Take the wiper fluid to the snowplow driver, use it, and he'll tell you he needs exactly four liters. A screen will open up with the 10-liter bottle, a 5-liter cup, and the 3-liter dog dish you picked up in

Rodrick's room. You can use the cup and dog dish to help you measure out four liters in the wiper-fluid bottle. It's really just simple math. First, click on the bottle and then click on the dog dish to fill it up. That's ten minus three, which leaves seven liters in the bottle. You just need to pour out three more liters, but the dog dish is full. No problem! Click on the dog dish and then click on the cup to empty the dish into the cup. Now click on the bottle and dump out three more liters. Perfect! Now you're left with the four liters you need. The plow is ready to go, but the driver tells

you he's going to get a cup of coffee before he gets moving. You might as well use this time to check on Greg.

SLED RACE TO THE FINISH

Back at the Heffley house, Greg is still playing video games! You're doing all the work to find his brother while he does nothing. Open up the curtains in the house to get Greg out of his video game trance. He'll tell you that Manny is probably looking for his blanket, Tingy.

Head outside and you'll see Manny—driving past in the snowplow! He's heading for the laundromat. Go inside the Quik-Spin and you'll find Manny on the floor, reunited with Tingy at last. Greg will appear and tell you that you've all got to get home before his mom returns from work.

On the way back home, the Whirley Kids will pelt you with snowballs. If you and Greg work together, you can push a big snowball down the path, which will knock them over like bowling pins. But now you're nearly out of time. You'll have to take a wild sled race to the Heffley house. You get there just as his mom pulls into the driveway.

She thanks Greg for being so responsible, but you know the truth. Greg pays you back by giving you an Island Medallion.

INSIDE POPTROPICA

DID YOU EVER WONDER HOW A POPTROPICA ISLAND GETS MADE? HERE, FOR THE VERY FIRST TIME, YOU'LL GET AN INSIDE LOOK AT HOW THE MAGIC HAPPENS. IT ALL STARTS WITH A DREAM . . .

Step 1: The Idea

The creators of Poptropica think about what kind of adventure would be fun and challenging. The idea can come from an exciting period in history, a popular legend, or right from the imagination. If the team agrees it's a good Island, the gears start to turn.

Step 2: The Script

A writer takes the idea and turns it into a script. The script tells the story of what the player will encounter on the Island from beginning to end. It describes the characters and locations, maps out the challenges, and includes the dialogue that the player and characters will say in the game.

HA! HA! HA!

Step 3: The Backgrounds

When the script is finished, the creative team divides it into different tasks for each team member. First, the Island is broken up into scenes, and illustrators get to work creating those. They need to do research first. In Time Tangled Island, for example, there were a lot of historical locations. The illustrators had to make sure the Poptropica buildings matched the real ones.

Step 4: The Characters

Other artists will get to work designing the characters. Every Poptropica character has a similar style, but each one gets a signature costume and look.

Step 5: The Mini-Games

Artists and programmers work together to create the challenges that players will encounter. In Reality TV Island, there were twelve mini-games in addition to all the small challenges that happen in the first part of the story. That's a lot of programming!

Step 6: The "Cut Scenes"

Sometimes when you're on an Island, you can't control what's happening to your character and you watch the action almost like you're watching a movie. These moments are called "cut scenes," and they need to be handled separately.

Step 7: The Missing Pieces

As the Island starts to come together, the team may notice that some things still need to be worked out. Usually, new dialogue needs to be written. For example, a character might ask you for help. After you help them, they need to say something else when you talk to them again. When this missing dialogue is added, the Island is almost done.

Step 8: The Test

Team members test the Island and look for problems and glitches. They don't always find them all! Sometimes, players will find glitches after the Island is open, and the programmers have to go back in and fix them.

Step 9: The Promotion

Before an Island opens, the team starts to tease it on the Blog. A team member makes a short video so players can get a preview of the Island.

Step 10: The Big Day

The day an Island opens is an exciting day for the team. They'll often check the Blogs of Poptropica fans to see how the players like the Island.

✋Wait—

is this the end of the book? How can that be? There is so much more about Poptropica that we need to know.

Fear not, there's plenty more fun where this came from.

Head over to penguin.com/poptropica to find exclusive content.

Yes... We're OPEN